THE SACRED
SECRETION

YOUR GUIDE TO KUNDALINI ENERGY, CHRIST OIL, INNER ALCHEMY AND THE MONTHLY SEED.

Kelly-Marie Kerr

UKCS Registration Number: 284727422

www.seekvision.co.uk

ISBN 978-1-9164137-4-0

First Printing, 2023
Printed in the United Kingdom

DISCLAIMER:
This book contains general medical information only. Nothing in this book is intended to be a substitute for qualified, certified professional medical or psychological advice, diagnosis or treatment. You must NOT rely on the information in this book as an alternative to medical advice given by a professional healthcare provider or doctor. Consult a qualified professional healthcare provider or Medical Doctor (MD) with questions or concerns regarding practices or substances mentioned in this book that may affect your health or general wellbeing. You should always seek immediate professional medical attention if you think you are suffering from any medical condition. The medical information within this book is provided without any representations or warranties, express or implied. The medical information contained within this book is not professional medical advice and should not be treated as such. The medical information contained within this book is ONLY provided to highlight comparisons within the topics presented here, further personal research and professional guidance is always recommended.

THE SACRED SECRETION

CONTENTS

PART II – PRACTICAL GUIDANCE 77

ACKNOWLEDGEMENTS AND INTRODUCTION

Special thanks to <u>all</u> of the truth seekers and pioneer's past, present and future that have preserved and shared the sacred knowledge of inner alchemy, the three-fold enlightenment, sacred secretion and or kundalini rising throughout history. I am deeply grateful to all the writers, researchers, artists, musicians, adepts etc. who have sought to keep the sacred knowledge alive and kept the light of truth blazing powerfully. Goodness knows where humanity would be without their dedication, compassion, and expertise.

My first felt experience of the Sacred Secretion or Kundalini rising which I shared in **The God Design: Secrets of the Mind, Body and Soul** was deeply healing and positively transformational -- there really are no words to describe the incredible, replenishing sensation of utter renewal in and through my entire being... literally the light of love peeled through me and vibrated every cell and atom of my body into harmonic bliss! It was glorious and the waking visions I experienced were simply profound. This phenomenon truly is the blessing of all blessings and I sincerely hope that by shining a light on this freeing process more souls will be able to heal and experience true unconditional love for themselves.

The healing and the revival of energy through my body, thoughts, and emotions that I experienced and continue to experience have been the driving factor for all that I have researched, documented, and shared in my books, courses, and videos. These works decode biblical alchemy and other ancient symbols and metaphors with the aid of mystical insights and the corroboration of the latest scientific discoveries and theories in order to help the earnest seeker to have a clear understanding of their own potential.

The Sacred Secretion is the ultimate secret that lies behind every miracle, myth, and mystic experience... and... it lies within YOU.

The Sacred Secretion is the glorious biology within every individual that can give birth to a new "resurrected" human – *"Christ within, the hope of glory"* (Col 1:27 KJV). This can fulfil the prayer: *"Thy Will be done on Earth as it is in Heaven"* (Matthew 6:10 KJV).

This particular book pulls together all of the most prominent and integral information regarding the Sacred Secretion process and how YOU can embody this teaching for yourself.

It's entitled **The Sacred Secretion: Your Guide to Kundalini Energy, Christ Oil, Inner Alchemy and the Monthly Seed** because I've endeavoured to include all of the most beneficial information and practical knowledge from my previous books and videos, as well as new insights and truths, to create this overall or "best-bits" compendium of knowledge and guidance.

If you're looking to further your research, my previous book, **The God Design: Secrets of the Mind, Body and Soul** takes a deep dive into these esoteric teachings, shining a light on the various contexts and perspectives that the "Sacred Secretion" alchemy exists in throughout the ages.

For example, **The God Design** explores and explains the Sacred

Secretion in relation to Eastern Traditions such as Kundalini and Kaya Kalpa and newer religions such as Christianity, highlighting many Biblical metaphors. Plus, modern scientific contexts of the Sacred Secretion, such as Xxenogensis are described, as well as giving other insights into the anatomical process and practical advice.

Another title, **Elevation: The Divine Power of the Human Body** decodes the inner alchemical or biochemical process hidden within the Bible book of Revelation and gives a full transliteration of this wildly misunderstood writing. Ultimately illustrating the potential available to each and every one of us -- as it says in Psalms 82:6 says, *"you are ALL Gods and sons of the most High."*

Lastly, **"The Cell of Life: Awakening and Regenerating"** provides a full account of the "Jesus seed" or "Christ Lunar Germ" born in the solar plexus with every cycle of the moon and all of the mystic or esoteric anatomical symbols that correspond with the seeds journey.

For those of you who have read these previous titles you may notice some repetitions in this book, this was necessary in order to condense all of the fundamental facts and theories into this specific offering designed to encapsulate the inner alchemy as comprehensively, yet plainly as possible. There are many new insights and hopefully you will still enjoy the book regardless of whether you are new to the subject or are a seasoned student. It's always beneficial to receive a wonderful refreshment and reinvigoration knowledge, which helps to cement the knowledge deeply into your psyche until the fluency and application of these esoteric secrets become second nature.

It's an honour to journey with you all, may divine light manifest itself in you all, always and in all ways.

Namaste

PREFACE
What is the Sacred Secretion?

The **Sacred Secretion** process which is synonymous with Kundalini Energy and Christ Oil is also known as the **Great Regeneration, Super Consciousness Awakening** and the **Threefold Enlightenment.** It's called "threefold" because it causes changes in the body, mind, and spirit. Meaning that the benefits are felt:

- Physically
- Mentally
- Energetically

This book explains the inner alchemical process which in short, is a monthly opportunity for self-renewal and enlightenment (regeneration) and coincides with the cycles of the moon. You will come to see that this cycle has to do with the lymphatic-water system, stem cell development and proliferation (mitosis), nitric oxide production, and pineal activity (metabolism).

Pineal metabolism is essentially the pineal gland upgrading serotonin and melatonin into DMT and the **biochemicals of super consciousness** (which were also given in my book, **The God Design:**

Secrets of the Mind Body and Soul) and are discussed in various videos on my YouTube channel, "Kelly-Marie Kerr."

When the height of super consciousness awakening occurs, tingles are felt all over the body and there is an intense feeling of bliss which penetrates every facet of your being. After the initial wave subsides there is an indescribable feeling of newness and clarity body, mind, and soul.

Other effects include but are not limited to healing and cleansing on all levels, sharper foresight, and hindsight, increased cognitive abilities, new levels of enthusiasm and motivation, ideas and inspirations coming to you effortlessly, improved memory recall and focus, deeper empathy, and discernment i.e., you might continue to experience goosebumps or tingles when you hear spiritual truths and or feel a knowing twinge when you're exposed to lies. You'll also witness many divine synchronicities, a supreme upgrade in your abilities to manifest your dreams and desires and begin to notice your problems dissolving easily as you align with limitless power and grace.

> "There is an automatic procedure within the human body, which, if not interfered with will do away with all sickness, trouble, sorrow and death, as stated in the Bible."
>
> **Page 21, "God-Man: The Word Made Flesh" by George W Carey & Ines Eudora Perry**

The **Preservation of the Sacred Secretion** (Super Consciousness Awakening) is described by experts as THE GREATEST SECRET IN HUMANITY.

From culture to culture and age to age, all throughout history, this process has been taught and known by many coded names including:

- Manna from Heaven
- Merkabah Ascension
- The Alchemical Wedding
- Kundalini Rising
- 144 DNA Activation
- Clavis Rei Primae
- Xxenogenesis (nuclear fusion)
- Naronia
- The Crystalline Dew
- The Anointing Oil (Christ Oil)
- The Tibetan Rainbow body of Light
- The Christian Resurrection Body

All of these teachings correspond with the same underlying process of inner alchemy or Sacred Secretion preservation for **Super Consciousness Awakening.**

The basis for this teaching is the understanding or "inner" standing that IN you there is a consciousness that over comes the world which can be activated by the preserving and raising of the Sacred Secretion (inner alchemy). It is the "Christ" or "Super" self of you -- it is the genius or GENE-ius of you, the God-self of you that is the master within you and is the wholeness in you.

This process occurs every month when the moon is in your sun (zodiac) sign and encourages the regeneration of every cell of your being and even activates dormant brain cells. The ancients called anyone who had this experience a "Christ" (Anointed one).

With this introduction in place, it's important to understand why being aware of and monitoring your thoughts, emotions and exterior influences is paramount to successfully preserving and raising your own Sacred Secretion and reaching super consciousness.

AWARENESS
How Do Your Thoughts, Emotions, and Influences Affect Your Inner Alchemical Process?

All of the great masters have shared their insights on the power of thought and emotion. This is because water carries the imprints of our thoughts and emotions throughout our bodies, which is paramount since we are literally made up of 70% water.

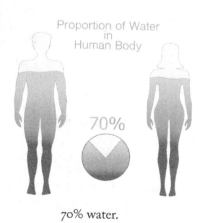

70% water.

Water, specifically in the lymphatic system carries and memorises our thoughts and emotions throughout the temple-body like a programme towards our health and radiance or disease and dreariness. Our billions of cells adjust according to these signals. Due to this mechanism, the quality of our thoughts and emotions effects the quality of our health along all lines and consequently the world around us.

The body always reflects the minds choices and is fully influenced by our thoughts and emotions. In other words, the lymphatic system creates the physical outcomes of our conscious and subconscious thoughts and emotions. Again, this is because thoughts and emotions are vibrations that leave imprints in our lymph water.

The other important thing to remember about the lymphatic water system as we continue is that EVERY SEED BEGINS ITS LIFE EXCLUSIVELY IN WATER -- **including ALL bodily stem cells and DNA!**

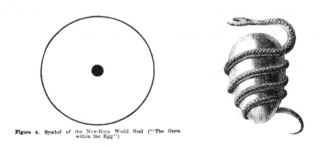

Figure 4. Symbol of the New-Born World Soul ("The Germ within the Egg")

Egg Symbolism.

> "The sign of the egg represents potentiality, the seed of generation (stem cell), the mystery of life."
> **Page 94, Dictionary of Symbols by J C Cirlot**

Stem cells are the beginning of the *physical* body and water is the medium for life. These two factors drive our potential to initiate the resurrection body. The potential of stem cells is fascinating, they have the ability to self-renew and become any cell in the body.

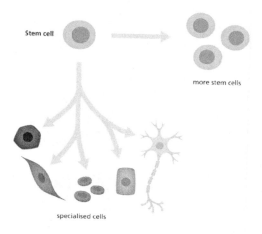

Stem Cell Production and Proliferation.

YOU ARE MADE OF CELLS, billions of them, and again every cell of your body, including DNA and stem cells start their life exclusively in water; the lymphatic-water system includes bone marrow (birthplace of blood cells), cerebrospinal fluid (CSF or Christ Oil), and the spleen.

So, one thing you must take away from this chapter is that your body and experience of reality is always being shaped by your thoughts and emotions – NO MATTER WHAT! At all times YOU are either perpetuating life, health and joy or death, disease, and misery.

So now that we've grasped this integral driving factor, let's discuss the actual process in a simple step by step guide.

A STEP BY STEP GUIDE TO THE INNER ALCHEMICAL PROCESS

THE PROCESS 1
The Timing and Quality of the Monthly Influx, "When the moon enters your zodiac sign."

There is a perpetual "Sacred Secretion" cycle occurring in the temple body. This inner alchemical cycle causes degeneration or regeneration physically, mentally, and spiritually depending on your vibration and choices.

Due to what's known as the monthly cranial respiration cycle, this cycle is governed by your fluidic (lunar) body which cycles coinciding with the moon.

Once every 29.53 days, when the moon enters the zodiacal constellation that you were born under and for approximately 3.5 days thereafter, there is an opportunity to preserve and raise your Sacred Secretion for **super consciousness awakening.**

At this appointed monthly time, you receive an astral influx of stellar (star), planetary and lunar energy that is specific to your atomic (astral) self.

This astral influx of bespoke cosmic energy is essentially "Light" in the form of photons (electromagnetic energy). Its quality differs for each zodiacal sign due to the atomic variables and potencies of the stars and planets in or near each constellation. It is the

differentiations within this energy that create the wonderful characteristics, talents, interests, and idiosyncrasies of each individual "self".

This astral influx is known as "solar seeds" in occultism and the
"solar wind" in modern science. Scientifically speaking, the earths
magnetosphere deflects the "solar wind" (a supersonic stream of
charged particles) toward earth. The solar wind is a plasma that
consists of charged atoms, originally formed by photons. Under a
microscope it can be seen that photon-light-particles have the form
of what's known as the "seed of life" in sacred geometry. The "Seed
of Life" is made up of seven interlocking circles also known as the
"Genesis Pattern" and coincides with the cross section of DNA.

Genesis Pattern seen in photon light (seed of life).

DNA Cross Section.

The size of the moon (crescent to full) affects the concentration of the astral influx also. You receive your unique astral influx monthly via the Earth's satellite, the moon (which acts as a giant reflector for cosmic rays to reach you).

The reason the opportunity for super consciousness awakening happens monthly is due to the moons orbit reacting with the magnetite crystals in your brain.

When the moon travels through the same position that it was in at the time of your birth, the *astral influx* contains the same influences, or energies that were presented to you or installed into you from or by Source (God) at the time of birth.

Your individual *astral influx* is totally bespoke and depends on your birth time, place, and day. So, when the moon traverses through your specific zodiacal sign each month, you receive an injection of life – totally custom to you! If you follow and embody the teachings of enlightenment, this injection of bespoke *astral influx* can optimise your abilities, flush all of your systems and help you know yourself more clearly.

"When the Moon, in the course of her motion, arrives at the same point during each month, she impregnates these "seeds" and endows them with magnetic life; therefore, in an occult sense, she confers upon humanity the powers and possibilities of magical forces. It is this Luni-Solar influx of Naronia within the human body that controls the real foundation and basis of spiritual development and occult power."
(Page 126) [Naronia] "Light of Egypt" by Thomas H. Burgoyne

For the sceptics among you let's take a look at how all of this is scientifically plausible. In Quantum physics, the *Implicate Order* says that the physical, psychic, and spiritual (invisible or energetic) realms are ultimately connected. It is this connection that leaves us susceptible to various combinations of energetic stellar, planetary, and lunar influences. The Implicate Order offers a holistic account of the human being and his environment, it explains the reception of information from the environment not only via sense receptors, **but also through every cell of the human organism as organic piezoelectricity.** You can also watch my YouTube video about the Monthly Cranial Respiration cycle for further scientific corroboration.

Having looked at the characteristics and potential of the monthly astral influx we can now discover **how to calculate our correct Sacred Secretion practice time.**

Some of you may be aware that there is more than one system for following astrological movement. So, which is the correct system to follow and why?

The answer is both **tropical and sidereal:**

- The *Tropical Zodiac* is the position of the sun referenced against the earth's horizon.
- The *Sidereal Zodiac* is the position of the sun referenced against the stars.

Both of these systems can be compared against one another, when represented as wheels they can be superimposed using the sun as the common point. This alignment makes one comprehensive calculator, showing **us that the imprint or "shadow" of the sidereal zodiac on the earth gives us the tropical zodiac!**

This is why BOTH systems are used in Biodynamic Agriculture, and why BOTH systems should be used to find your super consciousness awakening (Sacred Secretion) practice time.

During the tropical timing you will be preparing your vessel (body) as the moon glides through the outskirts of your zodiac, and during the sidereal time you will be poised for the great regeneration. In the book GOD-MAN: The Word Made Flesh, Dr George Carey also highlights the importance of the tropical/sidereal overlap:

> *"These designing schemers supressed the truth in order to stop people from realising what is meant by "the heavens declare the glory of God." The moon, in its monthly round of 29.5 days enters the outer stars of a constellation (tropical) 2.5 days before it enters the central stars of the constellations (sidereal) that are known as the signs of the zodiac.* **But to this day the whole anti-Christ world go by tropical system that makes the moon enter a sign of the zodiac 2.5 days before it does enter it and thus perpetuates a lie!"**

The tropical system is indeed approximately 2.5 days ahead of the sidereal system, but the difference between the two systems is a simple matter of space, distance, and perspective. Again, **both** bear relevance in our temple body's due to the hermetic law of correspondence (implicate order). So, you must do your super consciousness awakening practice when the moon is moving through your zodiacal sign on **both the tropical and sidereal calendars.**

I have created a calendar which is available on amazon and in other bookstores called **The ReGENEration Calendar** which gives you your specific Sacred Secretion times at a quick glance. If you find videos easier to follow, I have a short 5-minute YouTube video on my channel "Kelly-Marie Kerr" which explains how to calculate your own times. For everyone else, I will explain the process of finding your time-phase for yourself now.

Calculate Your Sacred Secretion Timing

1. Use your birthday to find out your TROPICAL birth (sun or zodiac) sign according to this list:
   - Aries (March 21 - April 19)
   - Taurus (April 20 - May 20)
   - Gemini (May 21 - June 20)
   - Cancer (June 21 - July 22)
   - Leo (July 23 - August 22)
   - Virgo (August 23 - September 22)
   - Libra (September 23 - October 22)
   - Scorpio (October 23 - November 21)
   - Sagittarius (November 22 - December 21)
   - Capricorn (December 22 - January 19)
   - Aquarius (January 20 - February 18)
   - Pisces (February 19 - March 20)

2. Use a TROPICAL calendar or App such as Deluxe Moon to find out when the moon is next moving into your birth (sun or zodiac) sign.

3. Use a SIDEREAL calendar or App to find out when the moon is next moving into your birth (sin or zodiac) sign. Deluxe Moon App is great because it has both a tropical mode and a sidereal mode, so you can get both time phases from one place.

4. Now add the two durations together. **This is your full and correct Sacred Secretion practise time.** You will find that the

tropical phase is a couple of days in duration, the sidereal phase is a couple of days in duration and that when you add the two time-phases together you have a period 3.5-5 days long.

For example, if Deluxe Moon has the moon entering **tropical Pisces on the 7th of October this is when you should START your practice. Then find the day when the moon leaves **sidereal** Pisces (11th of October) -- this is when you can FINISH your practice.

AGAIN, the tropical timing comes immediately before the sidereal timing – you will need to do your **regeneration practice** for the entire duration of both systems to maximise your potential. **YES, this means doing your practice for the tropical days AND the sidereal days.**

To summarise what we've covered in this chapter, the combined energies of distant planets, stars and our nearby sun are what the moon reflects into our human organism every 29.53 days. You can calculate your own time using the steps above, by watching the designated YouTube video or by purchasing The ReGENEration Calendar which has all the time-phases readily laid out for you.

THE PROCESS 2
The Light (Astral Influx) is Received by the Claustrum and Splits into the Pituitary and Pineal Glands

During your appointed Sacred Secretion time phase, the "Light" (bespoke astral influx) comes through the "door of brahma," also known as the fontanelles. In early Christian mysticism, this opening was known as "Thura Iesous," -- the door of Iesous (Jesus).

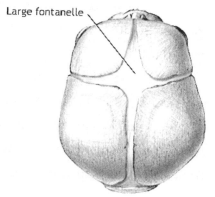

Large fontanelle

Fontanelle, connection point.

It is then received by the claustrum, a blood/cerebrospinal fluid (CSF) barrier. Neurons inside the claustrum branch out and extend around the entire circumference of the brain, much like a "Crown of Thorns." Research shows that the claustrum can act like an on-off switch for consciousness.

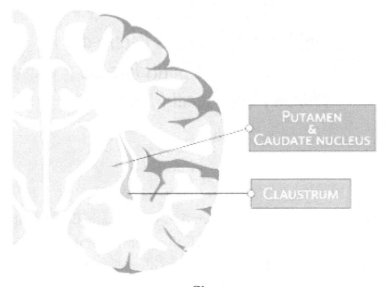

Claustrum.

Dr Carey says, *"It is from the claustrum that the wonderful 'Christ oil' is formed."* In plain terms, the "Light" acting on the substances of the brain forms cerebrospinal fluid (CSF) also known as "Christ Oil".

In the body there is a continual exchange occurring between blood, CSF, sexual vital essences, and lymph -- the moon regulates all of these vital fluids. CSF is saline (salty) and alkaline, meaning electron (life force) rich. It is secretly known as the *"blood of the Lamb."* The CSF ventricles are even shaped like ram horns.

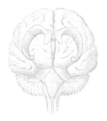

CSF, Christ Oil, The Blood of The Lamb/Ram

CSF IS THE MOST SUBTLE AND ELECTRICALLY CHARGED FLUID IN THE BODY, The breath (mostly nitrogen 777 and oxygen 888) charges CSF. **Super consciousness awakening (preserving and raising the Sacred Secretion) relies on the charging and transmuting of this subtle fluid.**

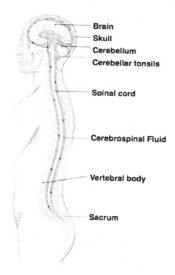

CSF, Christ Oil flow, cycle.

Here are a couple of quotes that will help you inner-stand the magic and potential of CSF.

> "The human brain is surrounded by a subtle humidity (CSF), which causes an akashic precipitation, a brain 'dew' which is more of a luminous ether than a liquid. This 'dew,' however, is more tangible than a gas, and as the manna is said to have fallen from heaven, so this 'dew' of thought trickles down between the two hemispheres of the cerebrum and finally fills the third ventricle, which is the reservoir of this heavenly water. This 'dew' carries in suspension, or as the alchemists might say, is 'tinctured' by the mental activity of the seven brain stars which form the northern constellation of man. Paracelsus thus sums up the mystery: **The whole of the Microcosm is potentially contained in the Liquor Vitae, a nerve fluid—in which is contained the nature, quality, character and essence of beings.'"**
>
> **(Page 73) [Salt of the Wise] "Nitrogeno 03: Making Gold" Autumn 2016, Fontana Editore**

> "The kundalini utilizes that which is termed spinal liquid. It actually ionizes CSF and changes it molecular structure and consequently the basic DNA structure of the entire body."
>
> **Page 243, A Beginners Guide to Creating Reality by Ramtha**

Dr Zappaterra's experiments confirmed that CSF is the conveyer of Light energies (astral influx) in the body. **Yes, this means that the monthly astral influx precipitates in the body as CSF (Christ Oil).**

After the "Light" precipitates as CSF in the claustrum, it is differentiated into two distinct potencies by the pituitary gland and the pineal gland. The different hormones and vibrational qualities of the pituitary and pineal enable this division.

The two potencies are esoterically known as black kundalini (pituitary) and white kundalini (pineal) or "lunar" (fluid) and "solar" (fire/mineral) respectively.

THE PROCESS 3
What are the Two Potencies Formed by the Pituitary and Pineal Glands?

First, we have the **pituitary potency**, also known as the lunar potency, lunar germ, or lunar seed.

Flowing into the pituitary CSF becomes magnetic, "female", in its quality and action. Some secret names for this potency are:

- "Oil/Water of Life"
- "The feeling principle"
- "Soul – Fluid Body"
- "Silver" or "Milk"

But what exactly is the "lunar germ" according to modern science?

The answer is protoplasm (also known as cytoplasm and soma).

This "lunar fluid" is present in EVERY cell of the body. In the Secret Teachings of All Ages, Manly P Hall explains that protoplasm is *"not only the structural UNIT with which all living cells start life, but with which they are subsequently built up…"*

Second, we have the **pineal potency**, also known as the solar potency, solar germ, or solar seed.

Flowing into the Pineal CSF becomes electric, "male", in its quality and action. Some secret names for this potency are:

- "Fire of Life"
- "The thinking principle"
- "Spirit – Fire Body"
- "Gold"
- "Honey"

But what exactly is the "solar germ" according to modern science?

According to the majority of experts on this subject, the answer is nitrogen, previously known as the alchemists "fire of life" or "kundalini".

Nitrogen has 7 protons, 7 neutrons and 7 electrons (777) **and it forms minerals (cell-salts) in the body. Without Nitrogen cells cannot be generated.**

Dr Carey's opinion on the nature of the "solar pineal potency" is slightly different, he stated that the "solar germ" is electrons (of which nitrogen has 7). Of course, electrons combine to form atoms such as nitrogen. The other predominant source of electrons or life energy in the body is phosphorus, previously known as the alchemists "light of light."

Interestingly, phosphorus is part of the nitrogen family and also forms minerals (cell-salts) that generate cells in the body.

To summarise, the pituitary potency is protoplasm (also known as cytoplasm and soma) and the pineal potency is electrons – predominantly taking form as nitrogen "fire" and phosphorus "light" atoms, which subsequently forge minerals (the cell-salts that build the cells of the body).

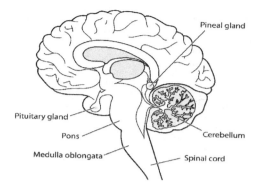

Pituitary and Pineal, both secrete their
potencies into the 3rd CSF Ventricle.

THE PROCESS 4
The Pineal and Pituitary Streams Merge in the Spleen to Produce the "Seed."

This part of the inner alchemy is little understood, but those who are familiar with the Sacred Secretion will know that it was George Carey in **God-Man: The Word Made Flesh** who highlighted the "birth" of the monthly "Jesus Seed" in "Bethlehem", the house of breads or solar plexus,

> "Every 29.5 days a **"seed"** is born in, or out of the solar plexus – the oil (pituitary potency) unites with the mineral salts (pineal potency) and thus produces the monthly seed which goes into the vagus."
>
> **Page 90, GOD MAN: The Word Made Flesh by G W Carey**

But what is the scientific evidence for this "seed" and what is its role in the preserving and raising of the Sacred Secretion for super consciousness awakening? Let's take a closer look.

The pituitary and pineal streams flow down from the brain through the left and right sides of the autonomic nervous system, these channels are also known as the Ida and Pingala Nadis. They then continue through the semilunar ganglion, esoterically known as the "sea of Galilee" which carries the two potencies or streams to the solar plexus which innervates the spleen.

In the spleen the two potencies merge and "conceive" or generate the seed in the spleen.

> "...The spleen mysteriously creates cells, it does this by enclosing a minute body from the cerebrum within a case (Moses' basket). Thus, within the spleen is formed the TRUE PHYSIOLOGICAL SEEDS (CELLS) OF THE BODY..."
> **Page 111, Zodiac, and the Salts of Salvation by G W Carey**

The spleen is where we find the modern scientific parallel of this historical symbolic description. The spleen is part of the lymphatic-water system, it contains the all-important germinal centre, symbolically known as the "manger", this is where *"Jesus"* is born (*"Jesus is a germ/seed of life"* G W Carey).

The spleens germinal centre is a site of multipotent stem cell production. **Therefore, the esoteric "Jesus Seed/Germ/Cell" is parallel with water born stem cells generated by the union of the pituitary-lunar potency and the pineal-solar potency.**

Multipotent stem cells are infant cells which have the ability to become many types of bodily cells, thus through their production we are replenished, invigorated, and renewed at a cellular level (from the inside out).

Let's take a look at how the two potencies combine to form the seeds or cells of life:

- The solar-pineal potency (nitrogen and phosphorus) forms the nucleoli and nucleus of cells i.e., the central part.
- The lunar-pituitary potency (protoplasm or soma) forms outer body of cells.

Anna Kingsford describes this process poetically on page 144 of **The Perfect Way,**

> *"In her bosom (protoplasmic lunar-body), is conceived the bright and holy Light, the Nucleoli."*

In the diagram below, the "SOLAR GERM – Electric, pineal potency" is "c/d" and the "LUNAR GERM – Protoplasm, pituitary potency" is "a/b". Together these two essences form stem cells or the "Jesus seed" born in the solar plexus every 29.5 days.

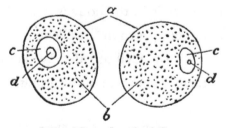

Cells of Round or Oval Form.
a, Border of the cell or cell-wall; b, cell substance;
c c, nuclei; d d, nucleoli.

The pituitary and pineal potencies combine to produce stem cells.

This inner alchemical sacred secretion process is parallel with the bodies monthly cellular mitosis.

Professor Hotema was referring to this process when he said,

> "The Spirit, a fiery nucleus (pineal potency) of noetic intelli-
> gence, is plunged into the fluidic habitat of a body of watery
> flesh (pituitary potency)."
>
> **Page 48, The Son of Perfection (Part 1) by H Hotema**

When explaining how cells operate and preserve themselves, Professor Hotema said,

> *"The cytoplasm (protoplasm) of the cell surrounding the nucleus is the negative (lunar–alkaline) element. The nucleus is the positive (solar–acid) element. THIS MAKES THE CELL (seed) A BIPOLAR MECHANISM and the acid–alkali balance is imperative for life."*

In short, EVERY cell is bi-polar (luni-solar / pituitary-pineal potency based) and the production and proliferation (mitosis) of **physiological stem cells** in the body is what the masters once referred to as "Jesus" being born in "Bethlehem."

My previous title, "**The Cell of Life: Awakening and Regenerating**" provides further context and information regarding the divine "seed."

This particular book pulls together all of the most prominent and integral information regarding the Sacred Secretion process and how YOU can embody this teaching for yourself.

It's entitled **The Sacred Secretion: Your Guide to Kundalini Energy, Christ Oil, Inner Alchemy and the Monthly Seed** because I've endeavoured to include all of the most beneficial information and practical guidance from my previous books and videos, as well as new insights and truths, to create this overall or "best-bits" compendium of knowledge.

My previous book, **The God Design: Secrets of the Mind, Body and Soul** takes a deep dive into these esoteric teachings, shining a light on the various contexts and perspectives that the "Sacred Secretion" alchemy exists in throughout the ages.

For example, **The God Design** explores and explains the Sacred Secretion in relation to Eastern Traditions such as Kundalini and Kaya Kalpa and newer religions such as Christianity, highlighting many Biblical metaphors. Plus, modern scientific contexts of the Sacred Secretion, such as Xxenogensis are described, as well as giving other insights into the anatomical process and practical advice.

Elevation: The Divine Power of the Human Body decodes the inner alchemical or biochemical process hidden within the Bible book of Revelation and gives a full transliteration of this wildly misunderstood writing. Ultimately illustrating the potential available to each and every one of us -- as it says in Psalms 82:6 says, *"you are ALL Gods and sons of the most High."*

For those of you who have read these previous titles you will notice some repetitions, but this was necessary in order to condense all of the highlights into this specific offering. There are many new insights and hopefully you will still enjoy the book and receive a wonderful refreshment and reinvigoration knowledge.

THE PROCESS 5
The Seed is Either Wasted or Preserved and Raised.

> "The germs of life, take on human form as they enter the stomach and spleen. Then, at the second stage, these human cells are taken down (fall) by Saturn into Tartarus (hell). Meaning that in the organs of procreation they are conjoined with "animal germs" (procreative "goat" germs).
>
> **Page 285, The Zodiac, and the Salts of Salvation by G W Carey**

Next, the seeds journey descends through the vagus (pneumogastric) nerve to the intestines and procreative organs, so this chapter is dedicated to those areas. It's important to discuss DNA synthesis and the magic of water at this juncture also.

From the spleen, some of the seed will automatically flow up the spinal cord from T12, expert Harold Percival calls this **"automatic reclaiming"**. The other part descends to the procreative (sexual) region of the body.

T12 (thoracic vertebrae 12) marks the **centre** of the human organism, it is the centre of the inner star or wheel of life.

T12 is the place where the solar plexus meets the spinal cord via the semilunar ganglion, it is also the point where the spinal cord narrows into "Sodom and Gomorrah." At this junction, the higher forces raise a portion of the seed up the spinal cord, and the lower forces pull the seed down toward the genitals, where there's an opportunity for **"voluntary reclaiming."** Meaning that you can choose to preserve and raise the seed from this point via the retention of sexual essences.

Another important point to observe about T12 is its link with DNA formation -- T12 is esoterically known as "Gilgal." The metaphysical dictionary tells us that Gilgal means "whirlwind." Esoteric studies show that the "whirlwind" symbolises the DNA double helix formed by the sacred geometry of the ratcheting dodecahedron in the pre-existent invisible light realm.

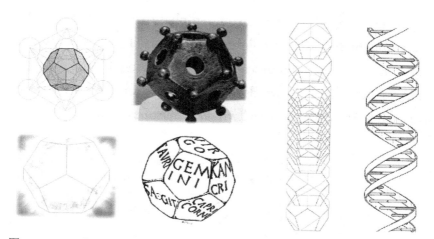

The turning dodecahedron of the light world forms the whirlwind or helix structure of DNA as it manifests into the physical world.

This is why the dodecahedron is considered "the ascension vehicle," because water born DNA and its dodecahedral scaffolding is the master of transformation. As proven by epigenetics our thoughts can rewrite our genetic DNA codes. This is why the 144,000 DNA Gene activation is analogous with the Sacred Secretion – as we preserve and raise the Sacred Secretion we simultaneously and inevitably override useless DNA programmes.

DNA is the same for all species -- the genetic information of roses, bacteria, animals, and humans is all being coded by the nitrogen (fire) bases and phosphorus (light) structure of DNA. EVERY CELL IN THE WORLD CONTAINS DNA -- and every cell is filled with salt water. In many cultures it is a spiritual belief that salty ocean water is the essence of all life. We could also use the analogy of spiralling serpents (DNA) being born in the ocean (lymph).

Before continuing on, let's reiterate the absolute magic of water. Water emits light (photons / electromagnetic energy), it is an electromagnetic dipole, meaning that it's both positively charged and negatively charged: Therefore, your **lymphatic (water) system is also electromagnetic – it is your light-energy body!** The Lymph System is the gateway for communication between blood, CSF, and sexual vital essences – in other words the sacred secretion is predominantly powered by the lymph system. Lymph simply means "water" in Greek.

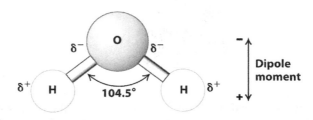

Water Molecule H2O, both positively and negatively charged.

Everything in the body is made of cells. All generation and degeneration of the body happens at the cellular level -- **The lymphatic water system maintains the health of the entire cellular terrain.** Its movement is **upward, towards the neck, against the force of gravity.** Again, our bodies are 70% water, and the lymphatic system is the most extensive system in the body.

When the lymph system is compromised there will be a change in the bodies pH. **pH stands for potential Hydrogen, which basically refers to the volume of electrons (life force energy) available.**

This is why the lymphatic system and our body's pH level (acid to alkaline) is so important!

- What is acid? Acid is devoid of free electrons.
- What is alkali? Alkali is electron rich.

So, our body should be slightly alkaline. Life Force energy is electrons born from photons. Electrons are teeny tiny magnets holding the cells of the body together, maintaining life and slowing degeneration. Electrons create atoms, atoms create molecules (cell-salts), molecules create cells, cells create tissues, tissues create organs, organs organise into systems, and... systems organise to create the body (organism).

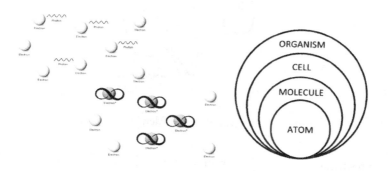

Photons forming electrons, forming atoms and so on...

Water transforms according to the vibrational frequencies emitted in its atmosphere. Gratitude, love, and musical harmonies improve the molecular structure of water, whereas negative, violent, or hateful emotions and sounds distort it (as within, so without). If you haven't seen or read about Masuro Emotos water experiments, then you absolutely must! As stated earlier, literally EVERYTHING that we are exposed to (via self and other) creates imprints on our lymph-water body.

Before the seed reaches the procreative region its passes through the stomach and intestines, esoterically known as the "alchemists alembic (bottle)" or the "vas hermetic (hermetic vase)".

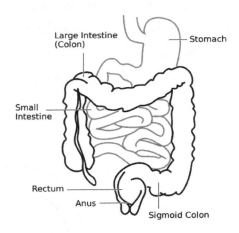

Stomach and Intestines, the Alchemist Alembic.

The stomach and small intestines are the vessels in which the sustaining minerals of life are prepared (these support the "birth of the seed" in the spleen). Without digestion the inner alchemical process is not possible. Digestion sets the vital mineral cell-salts contained in food free, creating a mineral base for the body. This mineral base is carried into circulation throughout the rest of the body via absorption into the blood and lymph at the small intestines.

Speaking on digestion, Dr Carey warns that the seed can be ruined by, "*alcoholic drinks, or gluttony that causes ferment-acid and even alcohol in the intestinal tract—thus "No drunkard can inherit the Kingdom of Heaven.*" Historically, the essence produced by digestion in the small intestine was known as "First Matter," "Lac Virginis" or "Prima Materia". It is described as an "oily water" or "fatty lymph". It supplies the blood with energy derived from food.

First Matter is comprised of the common elements – Carbon, Hydrogen, Nitrogen, Oxygen, and Phosphorus (CHNOP); all the constituents of DNA. Nucleic acids (DNA and RNA) are rich in phosphorus." The ancient alchemists believed that phosphorus was the "fifth element" – "Light" or "Spirit".

> 'Along with Earth, Air, Water, and Fire, the master alchemist recognized a fifth Element, a sort of philosophic secret, and this Element was that of Spirit or Light... Since phosphorous absorbs light and even glows with it, it is the agent in the body that absorbs the spiritual light.'"
> **Page 121, Esoteric Science Vol 1. J.S Williams**

You should recall from earlier in the book that phosphorus is part of the nitrogen family and that, phosphorus is alchemically considered to be "Light", while nitrogen is alchemically considered to be "plasma/fire." These two can be seen to produce life because again, they form the minerals or "cell-salts" that literally build cells and are fundamental parts of DNA.

DNA IS QUITE LITERALLY THE "QUINTESSENCE" of life! "Quint" means five, so DNA is the "five-essence" comprised of the five fundamental elements:

Elemental	State	Periodic Element
Earth	Solid	Carbon
Water	Fluid	Hydrogen
Air	Gas	Oxygen
Fire	Plasma	Nitrogen
Spirit	Light	Phosphorus

The word "phosphorus," meaning light-bearer in the early Greek Bible was translated to the word "lucifer" in the later Latin Bible, which has caused a myriad of delusions for the centuries that have followed. The number 666 has also been demonised but is simply the alchemist's carbon which has 6 protons, 6 neutrons and 6 electrons. There are many more examples of Bible misinterpretations in **Elevation: The Divine Power of the Human Body.**

The intestines also play a role in phosphorus absorption, Metaphysician Doctor Christlieb advised that,

> *"…the moral of this gospel of the flesh, is to produce plenty of phosphorus by means of good eating and drinking. Those who say, "Let us eat and drink, for tomorrow we die" are diametrically opposed to the Holy Scriptures."*

As explained earlier, "Chi" or "Life Force" is essentially "photon light" (electromagnetic energy), photons combine to form electrons and electrons combine to form atoms such as nitrogen and phosphorus which subsequently form minerals or "cell-salts" and DNA which programme, develop, proliferate, and differentiate stem cells. When the bodies pH level becomes too acidic phosphorus availability decreases.

Having covered T12, the stomach, and the intestines, we can now explore the transmutation that happens in the procreative region of the body which is esoterically known as "Sodom and Gomorrah."

Different organs of this lower region **work together** to process two types of procreative essences:

1. The prostate or skene's gland in women processes procreative/ sexual vital **fluid** (seminal fluid).

2. The gonads (testes and ovaries) process procreational **seeds/ cells** (sperm or ovum).

> *"The semen* **(fluid)** *is excreted by the Prostate as stated, and the Zoa* **(seeds)** *by the Gonads. The life Essence of the Body."*
> **Page 121, The Son of Perfection by H Hotema**

Experts say that these two, the fluids and the seeds don't combine unless ejaculation occurs.

The time which the seed spends in the organs of procreation is referred to as "hell" because of the torment induced by sexual temptation while the seemingly long task of **processing procreative essences** occurs.

Teachers from various cultures across the world, refer to the preservation of procreative essences in different ways. "Brahmacharya" is one guise. Guru Rajneesh of Rishikesh (home of kundalini yoga) says,

> *"Brahmacharya is a transmutation of the sexual energy, it is changing the whole energy from the sex centre to the higher centres. When it reaches the seventh centre samadhi happens. Learning and practicing the movement of vital energy is spiritual science..."*

Again, the procreative seed is processed in the ovaries and testes and the procreative fluid is processed in the prostate or skene's (periurethral) glands. If not outwardly released, these essences are reabsorbed by the body and become what Percival calls the fertile "soil" in the spleen i.e., the materials available for stem cell production.

Since the procreative essences are rich in electrons or life force energy (specifically nitrogen and phosphorus), minerals, and nutrients, "saving" it improves the quality and volume of the "soil" in the spleen, this is what's known as the "offering up of animals (procreative germs)."

If the "soil" in the spleen *is* enriched by the reabsorbed procreative essences, the cells produced there will be remarkable also. Thus, we have the regeneration of the body occurring under divine law.

Gnostics refer to the procreational essences, which become the furnishing product in the spleen as the **"salt of alchemy"** -- because all 12 cell-salts (minerals) exist within it. Samael Aun Weor warns us not to spill it, but to transform it — *"because mastery is represented in the salt of the earth, which is in our sexual secretions."* **Samael Aun Weor 1954**

Before we move forward, let's take a closer look at the two types of procreative essences.

The "Seed" Portion of Procreative Essences

Spermatogonia (seed) are the least mature form of "sperm," and ovum are the female equivalent.

Simply stated, they are stem cells. In their infant form they are pluripotent (still able to differentiate into a variety of different cell types).

> If preserved, the spermatogonia degenerate and their molecules are reabsorbed into the body – this is the true 10% tithe, *"The animal man actually robs his body of its cells (one tenth to be exact) in forming the germs of procreation. This is a fact which science will one day admit."*
> **Page 75, The Zodiac, and the Salts of Salvation by G W Carey**

The "Fluid" Portion of Procreative Essences

An oily substance is excreted by the Prostate, known as the Skene's in women, which varies in consistency, from a thin and volatile fluid to thick, fixed oil. The Skene's gland or "glands of skene" are also referred to as the periurethral glands, paraurethral glands and the female prostatic glands, this term highlights the functional similarity of the Skene's gland to the male prostate gland, as both produce fluids that contribute to sexual function and lubrication.

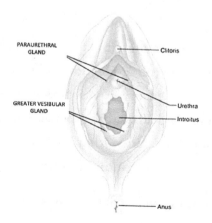

Female "Prostate" (Skene's/Paraurethral Glands).

This (fluid) portion of sexual substance is alkaline in reaction, rich in calcium, phosphorus, nitrogen, lecithin, albumen, nucleoproteins, iron, and vitamin E – it is remarkably similar to the fluids of the nervous system (CSF, interstitial fluid etc).

After seminal fluid is broken down in the prostate gland, and assuming it is not ejaculated it can be reabsorbed into blood and vital fluids where the body will prioritise the best use for it.

Professor Hotema states that, *"when the prostate and its "oil" act properly addictions can be dissolved."* The higher the quality and quantity of sexual vital essences, the more vibrant the Life Force sustaining the body.

This all equates to a practice revolving around the maintaining and honouring of Life Force and procreative essences. When the Life Force of the body becomes weak, the cells of the body cannot hold together properly, and this is evidenced as fatigue and other debilitating symptoms. Since procreative essences hold Life Force it is secretly regarded with the upmost importance.

By increasing the quality and quantity of procreative essences through retention and transmutation, Life Force and bio-magnetism intensify thus heightening cell production and repair. Subsequently, all aspects of health and sensory experiences including energy, joy, focus, clarity, memory, and adaptability become heightened.

In terms of modern science, there are at least five known measurable benefits of the retention of procreative essences:

1. **Increased Serotonin levels** - Serotonin is vital for inner DMT production (more about this later).
2. **Decreased Prolactin levels** -Excess Prolactin can cause various problems such as: depression and mood swings, anxiety, head-aches and even weight gain.

3. **Balanced Dopamine levels** - Too much dopamine drives addiction, compulsion, and aggression whereas too little dopamine leads to apathy and the inability to love. However, a "normal" level of dopamine fuels healthy motivation, focus and excitement for life.

4. **Increased Testosterone levels** - Good levels of testosterone promote healthy hair, skin, and teeth - not to mention the mental benefits; self-confidence, focus and determination.

5. **Increased brain Androgen Receptors (AR's)** - Androgen receptors allow your body to use testosterone.

My books, **THE GOD DESIGN: Secrets of the Mind, Body and Soul** and **ELEVATION: The Divine Power** of the Human Body include more information about "NOFAP", semen retention and the procreative essences.

To summarise, the "seed" descends to the procreative organs where it can be preserved and reabsorbed into the body providing a powerful mineral base (soil) for the production and repair of cells.

THE PROCESS 6
The Heart and the Baptism

If the procreative essences are preserved and reabsorbed as described in the previous chapter, then the next section of the inner alchemy is as follows: through what Harold Percival, author of the prolific book **Thinking and Destiny** calls "voluntary reclaiming", the vivified "seed" begins its ascension to cervical vertebrae 4 (C4) where the "baptism" takes place.

On its path to C4 it travels through other vital organs including the kidneys, pancreas, and the heart, so let's take at look at these wonderful body parts and their role in this phenomenal process.

The kidneys are esoterically represented by the Biblical place "Naphtali", Percival surmises that it is during the third week of your personal lunar cycle that the "seed" rises from the procreative region and into the region of the kidneys.

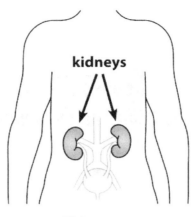

Kidneys.

The kidneys are regarded as the body's most important reservoir of "Life Force" energy, which again is photon-light transforming into electrons and precipitating as nitrogen (fire) and phosphorus (light):

> *"And I won't tell you the amount of dynamite we could make with all the nitrogen and phosphorus we could extract from a kidney."*
>
> **Page 70, "The Doldrums, Christ and the Plantanism" By B R Garcia**

The kidneys connection with the adrenal glands, means that fear, anger, hate, envy, insecurity, and other stressful emotions that cause increased cortisol and epinephrine secretions to toxify the body can diminish the "seeds" vibrancy. Poor memory, mind fog, fear, paranoia, and backache are all regarded as indicators of impaired kidney function and deficient kidney energy.

The kidneys also control the balance of bodily fluids and regulate the body's acid-alkaline pH balance, and we already know how important pH balance is toward regeneration due the bipolar, acid-alkaline, luni-solar nature of EVERY CELL IN THE BODY.

After the kidneys, the "seed" reaches the pancreas which is part of the endocrine and digestive systems. The pancreas secretes insulin. Insulin doesn't just control blood sugar; it also communicates with the DNA genes. In fact, insulin vitalizes DNA gene expression which aids what's known as the 144,000 light-body activation.

Eventually the "seed" reaches the heart centre and thymus gland, esoterically known as Jerusalem. The loves and hates of the mind are precipitated to this organ of emotion and are crystallized there. THIS IS REALLY IMPORTANT BECAUSE LOVE, COMPASSION, PEACE, AND FORGIVENESS ENLARGE THE HEART AND STIMULATE OXYTOCIN (OT) RELEASE BY THE PITUITARY, **THIS IS THE CHEMICAL CATALYST FOR PINEAL METABOLISM.**

These high-frequency emotions in the heart also cause CSF (Christ Oil) flow to increase and pressurize further assisting the pineal with its melatonin upgrades. Melatonin upgrades will be explained more thoroughly later.

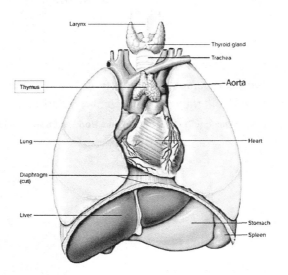

Heart Centre, Thymus and Thyroid.

Next, the "seed" continues upward from the heart centre and thymus to the throat centre and thyroid -- the place of "baptism."

Some of you will know that in the Bible it is "John" who baptises "Jesus" in the river Jordan, and some of you will also know that this is a metaphor for the biological process that happens to the "seed" in this region of the body.

In **The Tree of Life,** Doctor Carey wrote,

> *"Jesus was baptised of John in the fluids, the Christ Substance of the spinal cord."*

He also says that the word "John" is a chemical formula. Let's unpack this... "Jesus" is said to be 30 years old when "John" baptises him. Jesus's 33 years of life symbolise the 33 vertebrae in the human spine, therefore we know that Jesus's 30th year must correspond with the 30th vertebrae of the spine. The 30th vertebra of the spine is C4, the 4th cervical vertebra. C4 is also the site of the "cranial pump," known in Chinese medicine as Yui-Gen or the jade pillow pump,

> "CSF flows around the brain and spinal cord by two pumping mechanisms; the occiput (cranial pump by C4) at the top of the spinal cord and the sacral pump at the bottom."
> **Page 49, The God Design: Secrets of the Mind, Body and Soul by Kelly-Marie Kerr**

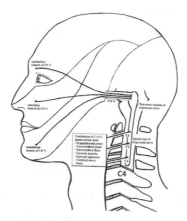

Cervical Vertebrae 4, C4 corresponding with the thyroid and occiput.

The top of the thyroid gland is level with C4. The Thyroid uses iodine (an electron donor) to produce thyroxine -- a powerful hormone which disinfects all the channels of the nervous system while we sleep! Without this biological iodine we would not be able to live.

In other words, thyroxine literally baptises (purifies) the body, mind, and soul... AND... the letters which spell John (previously Iohn in the Greek Bible) are found in the chemical formula of thyroxine.

Thyroxine

	Invisible, Creative Element, Astral Substance	Explanation
J/I	IODINE	There was no letter "J" in the Hebrew language, historically the name "John would have begun with an "I" or a "Y".
O	OXYGEN	Oxygen corresponds with the Hebrew letter "Aleph", the "catalyst of creation".
H	HYDROGEN	Hydrogen corresponds with the Hebrew letter "Mem", the "water of consciousness".
N	NITROGEN	Nitrogen corresponds with the Hebrew letter "Shin", the "fire of life". Aleph, Mem and Shin are known as the 3 mother letters.

In summary, this part of the Sacred Secretion process is where the "seed" (Jesus) is baptised by John (thyroid secretions).

THE PROCESS 7
The Vagus Crossing and the Cerebellum

3 "years" or vertebra after "his" or "the seeds" baptism at C_4, "Jesus" is crucified at age 33.

The 33rd vertebra is at the medulla, near the entrance to the cerebellum, where the **double cross of crucifixion (transmutation)** is situated.

The **double cross** is formed by:

1. The Ida and Pingala (left and right autonomic nervous system) And,

2. The left and right vagus nerves CNX (breath channels)

The "crucifixion" can actually be likened to an invigoration of power and or potential...

> "To crucify, means to add or to increase a thousand-fold. When electric wires are crossed, they set on fire all inflammable substances near them. When the Christed Seed crossed the nerve at Golgotha (Skull), the veil of the temple fell, and the generative cells of the body were quickened or regenerated".
>
> **Page 65, God Man: The Word Made Flesh by GW Carey**

But what does this mystical description really mean? Let's take a look. At the double cross in the medulla the "seed" is infused with air (nitrogen and oxygen from the vagus) which brightens and charges its Light in the same way that wind rouses fire and, the minerals (cell-salts) that protect the "seed" on its ascension are removed at the double cross.

> **The oil in the seed,** *when born, is covered by a crust of mineral salts, which, when baptized in Jordan by John, is loosened in order that the shell may fall apart when the seed goes over the cross, in order that the precious material may ascend into the pineal gland."*
>
> **Page 62, God Man: The Word Made Flesh by G W Carey**

After its "crucifixion" the seeds constituents enter the cerebellum which is symbolised by "Jesus's" tomb.

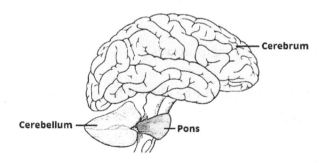

Cerebellum.

The cerebellum is the "intuitive brain," which controls the involuntary functions of the body, such as breathing, circulation, sleeping, digestion and swallowing (autonomic functions are basically all the functions that we don't really have to think about performing).

The cerebellum deals with synergistic activity and makes everything work in harmony with everything else. It is the coordinating activity of the cerebellum that allows us to perform whatever function we choose. All the activity of the body – muscle tension, joint relaxation, hearing, vision, the relationship of every part of the body in time and space – sends impulses to the cerebellum.

The cerebellum is like an electrical loom -- electrical impulses give the cerebellum a perfect representation of the body's position in time and space.

This powerful excerpt will tell us everything we need to know about the cerebellum,

> "The cerebellum clearly demonstrates the proper functioning of the intellect as it begins to move into Christ (super) consciousness. As we become aware of the underlying activity that coordinates, balances, and harmonizes every action in creation, the cerebellum begins to receive this picture. Then we have available to us the information that represents the total body of creation, and we can become co-creators with the primary Creator."
> **Revelation the book of Unity by J. Sig Paulson and Ric Dickerson – Unity Magazine May 1975, Vol 155. No 5, Page 9**

The Cerebellum is the part of the brain that receives messages from the nervous system, it tells us what we think or feel about certain things.

Eckhart Tolle explains that *"in the absence of awareness virtually all of your thoughts happen TO you instead of FOR you,"* meaning that the autonomous system is running riot and keeping you imprisoned to discordant thought patterns, thus you are not considered a "master of your-SELF".

When we give more power to the forebrain or rational part of our consciousness, we contribute to the atrophy and redundancy of the all-powerful cerebellum.

Consequences of the degenerate cerebellum:

- Unconsciousness during the transition between sleep and wake.
- **No recollection of astral experiences and difficulty remembering dreams.**
- Loss of reception between the body's higher and lower centers. Preventing the clarity of messages received from the Higher Self.

I recommend reading **The Cell of Life: Awakening and Regenerating** for more empowering information on the cerebellum. To recap, after the "seed" is crucified, it remains in the cerebellum (tomb) until it is "resurrected" or diffused through the cerebellar lingula.

Chapter summary: after its baptism by thyroxine the seed arrives at the double cross of Ida and Pingala and the Vagus nerve where it is crucified (increased in power 1000-fold) and subsequently travels to the cerebellum (tomb).

THE PROCESS 8
Super Consciousness Awakening (Resurrection).

After approx. 3 days (the time the moon spends in your individual sun or zodiac sign) the resurrected seed is released from the cerebellum, through the cerebellar lingula into the fourth CSF ventricle and the pituitary.

The resurrected seed causes the pituitary to secrete floods of oxytocin and vasopressin which consequently invigorates the pineal. The stimulated pineal then glows rich with nitric oxide and upgrades melatonin into **DMT and the other biochemicals of super consciousness awakening.**

The pituitary is the "master gland" of the endocrine system, the release of pituitary secretions corresponds with the electromagnetic radiation and the gravitational pull of the moon, this is possible due to the presence of magnetite crystals in the brain.

> "The pituitary gland is considered an important energetic organ, in that it contains magnetite, a magnetically sensitive compound."
>
> **Page 63, The Complete Book of Chakra Healing: Activate the Transformative Power by Cyndi Dale**

The two pituitary hormones that act as a major factor in the process and activation of Super Consciousness Awakening or Sacred Secretion are vasopressin (VP) and oxytocin (OT).

Vasopressin mediates stress and stabilises circulation. Vasopressin has the monumental task of maintaining the appropriate volume of water in the space that surrounds cells of the body, the extracellular matrix. This allows proper cellular function. In other words, vasopressin is indispensable to the lymphatic system, nervous system, and all other vital fluids (lunar aspect) of the body.

Oxytocin is the all-powerful hormone of love!

> "The moment oxytocin levels go up the brain's survival centres cool off. The amygdala **(an anagram for Magdalene)** slows the circuits of fear, sadness, pain, anxiety, aggression, and anger. Then the only thing we feel is a love for life."
> **The Reason Why Kindness Makes Us Happy, Unlimited Blog by J Dispenza**

Fear, sadness, pain, anxiety, aggression, and anger are all emotions that counteract super consciousness awakening, this is one of the reasons why I prefaced this book with some guidelines about thought and emotion control.

Oxytocin has many important roles in the temple body, including the stimulation, production, and mitosis of **stem cells!** Lack of oxytocin brings on premature aging, but increasing oxytocin levels through meditation, compassion and forgiveness actually slows the aging process by improving the behaviour of stem cells. The increased production and secretion of oxytocin causes a metabolic shift within the nervous system, from sympathetic (stress mode) into parasympathetic (restorative mode) - meaning a lowering of cortisol levels and faster healing of wounds. Oxytocin makes the heart swell which helps to heal the body from past hurts and traumas. In turn this provides a stronger capacity for forgiveness and unconditional love.

Perhaps the most important thing to remember about oxytocin is that it acts as a catalyst for pineal activity, thus producing the "felt sensation" of super consciousness awakening.

> "In the brain it first activates the pituitary, the feminine, negative pole, causing it to send a stream of **bluish** solar electricity thru the infundibulum to the pineal, the male, positive pole, thus completing the circuit."
>
> **Page 522, The Son of Perfection (Part 1) by H Hotema**

The "*stream of blue solar electricity*" travelling in the infundibulum between the pineal and pituitary that Hotema speaks of is nitric oxide (the sky is blue due to the presence of nitrogen).

The increased communication between the pituitary and pineal by nitric oxide is parallel with the continuous fusing and re-fusing of the two sides of the optic thalamus (joined inwardly by the Massa Intermedia and outwardly by the Fornix).

> This is the alchemical wedding; lunar (fluid) and solar (mineral) body's uniting in a climax of power and healing, in scientific terms the bodies electromagnetic circuit is balanced and thriving – this is what is meant in the book of Thomas where it says, "*Jesus said, if these two make peace*

with each other in this one house, they will say to the mountain, "Move Away," and it will move away."

Thomas Logia 48

As stated, the "climax" of enlightenment which occurs in the pineal gland and has two major aspects.

1. The stimulation of nitric oxide release (the kundalini fire)
2. The upgrade of melatonin into the biochemicals of super consciousness awakening.

These two operations are synchronous and will now be explained in clear detail.

Nitric Oxide

The pineal gland is bathed in highly charged cerebrospinal fluid (CSF).

The pineal contains the following:

- Calcite crystals that are piezoelectric
- Endothelial cells that generate nitric oxide (NO)
- Pinealocytes that mediate nitric oxide (NO) release.

As described earlier, when we are in a state of harmony and the fluids of the body are purified and charged, the pituitary gland secretes more oxytocin and vasopressin improving pineal metabolism. When this occurs, pineal calcite crystals vibrate more vigorously causing the rapid release of nitric oxide (kundalini fire) and **subsequently, the pineal is stimulated to upgrade melatonin into DMT and the other biochemicals of super consciousness awakening.** We'll look at the role of DMT and the biochemicals of super consciousness properly once we finish learning about nitric oxide.

NO (Nitric Oxide) is basically nitrogen + oxygen, it is a colourless gas that is **formed by the oxidation of nitrogen.**

Nitric oxide influences pineal metabolism (DMT synthesis).

Nitric oxide is essential for the metabolism of ALL CELLULAR REGENERATION.

Nitric oxide is a molecule of health – the more the better! The benefits of self-produced nitric oxide are prolific! For example:

- Nitric oxide is involved with everything from the binding and release of oxygen and haemoglobin, to inhibiting inflammation.
- Nitric oxide is even linked to the destruction of viruses, parasites and malignant cells in the airways and lungs.

Nitric oxide stimulates mRNA, the messenger of DNA. Nitric oxide is a free radical, this explains why the awakening process is about dissolving old structures (physically, mentally, and emotionally). When pituitary hormones stimulate the pineal to upgrade melatonin into DMT, the DMT stimulates photon-light emissions from DNA, therefore we actually "shine brighter."

In **The Biology of Kundalini** page 43, Jana Dixon says, *"Tingles and bubbles are always felt with increased kundalini flow… The tingles are associated with increased nitric oxide."*

"Air" is mostly nitrogen (777) and oxygen (888). Electrons in the air are the "Life Force" in the **"breath of life."** More than we breathe for "air" we breathe to take in Life Force in the form of the electrons as nitrogen and oxygen.

Nostril breathing increases nitric oxide in the body (hence all of the pranayama's that involve nasal breathing). In Hinduism a common mantra is OM, Christianity altered OM and created their "AMEN." Chanting OM boosts the production of Nitric Oxide (NO) in the body. In fact, most spiritual practices boost nitric oxide flow and release excess carbon dioxide.

Having taken time to appreciate the value of arousing the kundalini fire (nitric oxide) and its ability to stimulate pineal metabolism we can now learn about the actual biochemicals of super consciousness awakening.

DMT and the Biochemicals of Super Consciousness Awakening

Like the sun, the pineal wakes us up with its serotonin secretion and puts us to sleep with its melatonin secretion.

Serotonin and Melatonin are both precursors to DMT which is known as the "spirit" molecule.

Serotonin is known as the body's "feel good" hormone. It assists with many bodily functions including appetite control, mood, endocrine regulation, learning and memory.

Melatonin assists with the regulation of sleep-wake cycles, is a potent antioxidant and interacts positively with the immune system. Melatonin suppresses the adrenal "stress hormone" cortisol and therefore has a positive effect on mood, consequently slowly the aging process.

Excessive production of the stress hormones "Cortisol" and "Epinephrine" can cause brain damage and problems in all other parts of the body – since the secretions of these hormones are caused by emotion, IT IS SCIENTIFICALLY PARAMOUNT FOR

MENTAL AND PHYSICAL HEALTH TO BE PEACEFUL, LOVING AND FORGIVING.

Serotonin and Melatonin are the nectar (amrita) of life, "sero" means seed, and "mel" is the Greek word for honey. A glimpse at their chemical structures reveals the letters that spell honey.

Serotonin

Melatonin

Melatonin and serotonin increase DNA synthesis and induce mitosis (cell renewal).

Serotonin and melatonin are derived from "tryptophan." Looking at the tryptophan/DMT pathway really helps us understand the concept of melatonin upgrades.

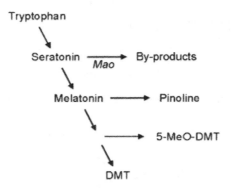

Tryptophan DMT Pathway

DMT is a self-produced hallucinogen which is the source of visionary light in transpersonal or "mystical" experiences.

> *"DMT in the pineal glands of biblical prophets gave God to humanity and let humans perceive parallel universes".*
> **Page 140, Conversations on the Edge of the Apocalypse by D J Brown**

But DMT does not and cannot work alone in the great regeneration! **A whole host of other blissful biochemicals are produced too, let's take a closer look at each of these incredible molecules.**

DMT - Dimethyltryptamine

Dimethyltryptamine is a self-produced psychedelic chemical commonly known as DMT. It gives rise to all of our dreams, imaginings, and visions.

DMT is prominently found in human Cerebral Spinal Fluid (CSF) and has the ability to harmonize the body's bioelectricity thus optimising cell health and activity.

As seen in the Tryptophan - DMT pathway illustration, DMT is a naturally occurring tryptamine derived from the amino acid Tryptophan, as are serotonin and melatonin.

The difference between Melatonin and DMT is minute. In fact, the only difference in their molecular structures is one atom of carbon and two atoms of oxygen which is equal to just one molecule of carbon dioxide.

Simply stated:

MELATONIN − CARBON DIOXIDE (CO2) = DMT

Mildly reduced carbon dioxide levels elevate brain and lung pH levels causing pH dependent enzymes to encourage endogenous (self-produced) DMT formation. So, as well as high-frequency thoughts and emotions, reducing our internal carbon dioxide aids super consciousness awakening too. Carbon dioxide levels are easily reduced by proper breathing and diet. For example, deep breathing such as is used in meditation decreases carbon dioxide, but over-eating raises it.

TRYPTOPHAN

We've seen that tryptophan is the precursor to DMT, but let's explore a little further! Tryptophan is an essential amino acid available only from food. Pumpkins, walnuts, and oats are among the best vegan sources. Tryptophan assists with nitrogen balance and creates niacin, which is essential in creating serotonin, melatonin and of course, the spirit molecule Dimethyl**tryptamine** (DMT).

In "Tryptophan: Structure, Sources and Side Effects" Danielle Haak says, *"When the body doesn't get enough tryptophan, it can't make serotonin, which leads to increased feelings of depression."*

PINOLINE

Pinoline is another factor in pineal metabolism. The hallucinogen Pinoline is a major contributor to the "felt" experience of enlightenment. The subconscious mind uses it to communicate with the deeper spheres allowing prophetic visions to be seen on the timeline. Lack of sleep inhibits pinoline production.

> *"When the kundalini (nitric oxide) hits the pineal gland it ionizes the spin ratio of serotonin, its electrons interchange altering its chemical nature. The molecule itself is reconfigured to its highest potential – pinoline."*
> **Page 255, A Beginner's Guide to Creating Reality by Ramtha**

Pinoline is also an extremely powerful, antimicrobial, anti-inflammatory, and anti-aging antioxidant.

The "pin" suffix in the word pinoline refers of course to pineal. Pinoline is a methoxylated tryptoline produced in the pineal gland during the metabolism of melatonin. The most amazing thing about pinoline is its ability to promote cell health and production in the nervous system (neurogenesis).

In "A Proposed Mechanism for the Visions of Dream Sleep", Dr Callaway speculates that the endogenous production of DMT and pinoline play a distinct role in dream phenomena. Funnily enough, these two fascinating compounds are also the major components of the shamanic treatment known as "Ayahuasca".

MEXAMINE

Scientifically is known as "5-Methoxytryptamine" (5-MT), Mexamine is also produced by the transmutation of melatonin in the pineal gland. Mexamine helps to decrease appetite and helps to repair nerve damage.

BENZODIAZEPINE

Commonly known as "benzos", benzodiazepine is a sedative that allows the mind and body to relax. It enhances the effect of the neurotransmitter "gamma-aminobutyric acid" (GABA) resulting in the secretion of other useful biochemicals that aid the body in rest, regeneration, and rejuvenation. Unlike synthetic benzodiazepine which is highly addictive and has many negative side effects, endogenous (self-produced) benzodiazepine is produced in precise doses for your individual needs.

TRYPTOLINE

Tryptoline is an antidepressant, it affects chemicals in the brain that may be unbalanced in people with depression. It is also a powerful antioxidant neurotransmitter and is chemically related to tryptamine.

LUCIFERIN

Known as the living-light (bioluminescent) molecule, luciferin increases the energy in the brain and nervous system and improves internal-mind-imagery. This makes dreams and visions very vivid, lucid, and luminous.

A luciferin is a generic term for a light-emitting compound with a bioluminescent reaction. For example, simple potassium salt is also known as a D-Luciferin. The energy needed for the basic reaction that produces light is taken from cellular ATP (adenosine triphosphate); oxygen binds to a luciferin molecule and forms a new molecule.

LIGHT IS THE BY-PRODUCT OF THIS REACTION

Japanese scientists Kikuchi and Kobayashi are the minds behind the proof of bioluminescence in humans. The process of bioluminescence requires the presence of two chemicals: luciferin and luciferase. When luciferin reacts with oxygen in the presence of luciferase, BIOLUMINESCENT, GLOW IN THE DARK LIGHT (oxyluciferin) is produced. This oxyluciferin is the luminous light emitted by all bioluminescent creatures (fireflies, jelly fish etc).

In other words, luciferin salts are light-emitting compounds that generate what is known as bioluminescence (living light).

> "At the molecular level, bioluminescence is produced when chemicals, or "substrates" intermingle at the right time and place: luciferin, luciferase, and a third player, oxygen."
> **Luminescentlabs.org**

To summarise this section about DMT and the biochemicals of enlightenment -- DMT and Luciferin etc., along with increased nitric oxide flow allows us to really "feel" the manifest experience of enlightenment. Luciferin is no doubt the cause of the "flashes of light" so often described by those who have had mystical experiences.

All of these enlightening biochemicals happen synchronously as part of the inner alchemical process known as preserving and raising the Sacred Secretion. This your God-given potential, to enhance melatonin within your body through your thoughts, emotions, actions, and behaviours. This phenomenon is a true gift and shows how "wonderfully made" (Psalm 139:14) we really are.

Before we conclude this section on super consciousness and the resurrection, we need to take another look at CSF (Christ Oil) because the foaming and seeping over of CSF effects the optic thalamus, third ventricle, and the massa intermedia in a profound way. Let's explore!

The biochemicals of super consciousness awakening enhance CSF, causing it to become "Amrita -- the nectar of the Gods" -- magnetized and charged (**ionized). Thanks to the spirit-fire cata-lyst (nitric oxide), CSF is multiplied (foams) and flooded with DMT, pinoline, and the other biochemicals of super consciousness as it seeps over the ventricles and bathes the entire body.

In the 2nd century Galen defined the "optic thalamus" as two oval masses closely associated with the CSF ventricles on either side of the brain. The two "oval masses" were named the "optic thalami" because they were found to be involved with the processing and **projections** of visual reality.

The optic thalamus is also known as:

- Ophthalmos or optanomai – "The eyes of the mind"
- Thalamus Opticus – The Latin form of "Couche Optique"
- Optic Eminence – a mystic synonym
- "The Holy Eye", "The Eye of Providence", "The Eye Which Sleepeth Not"
- "The Eye which is the subsistence of all things."

The front of the optic thalamus connects to the optic chiasma (above the pituitary) and the back connects to the epithalamus (including the pineal gland). So, the upgraded secretions from the pituitary and pineal directly affect it directly.

The Massa Intermedia is in the centre of the optic thalamus, it connects the two lobes of the optic thalamus, and in a way rules our very existence. Its surfaces form part of the walls of the **third CSF ventricle, esoterically known as the crystal cave or palace.**

"Reality" projects from the Massa Intermedia. At the Massa Intermedia is the centre of the brain's torus field, this centre point is a plane of inertia built by the brain's resonance. Our senses simply absorb and filter the frequencies that we project from the internal to the external back into consciousness and perceives them as "reality". The frequencies flow to the optic thalamus, where they are directed to the microcosmic sun (pineal) and the microcosmic moon (pituitary), allowing us to "see" our "reality".

The frequencies vibrate the cerebrospinal fluid inside the 3rd ventricle, giving rise to the shapes and forms of so-called "physical life". The entire experience of life is generated in this way. So, your creative power initialises in the Massa Intermedia and third CSF ventricle, and you can indeed write our own life stories. When you truly grasp this, dormant neurons light up creating new and powerful pathways of thought and possibility. This is a factor of the super consciousness awakening.

To recap, the biochemicals of super consciousness awakening travel from the pineal to the optic thalamus via the peduncles (two strands of nerve fibres). The optic thalamus, along with the 3rd ventricle receive the upgraded biochemicals, which has a "foaming affect" in CSF, causing it to rise and multiply.

When the supply of cerebrospinal fluid exceeds the volume of the central canal, and the ventricles of the brain it seeps over and bathes the nerves, resulting in the experience of an intense physical and spiritual bliss.

> *"Like yeast, the seed that comes fourth from the pineal,*
> **expands and causes the oil in the spinal cord to multiply."**
> Page 97, God Man: The Word Made Flesh by G W Carey

The ultimate clarity of mind occurs, the massa intermedia is freed from discordant cycles, limitless potential is realised, and the great regeneration is underway.

THE PROCESS 9
Thirteen Lunar Rounds

This chapter will explain the basics of the terminal filament which is said to be unlocked or opened after 13 lunar cycles of successfully preserving and raising the Sacred Secretion. According to Kundalini Energy theories, the terminal filament (filum terminale) is analogous with the lower part of the sushumna nadi and acts a conduit for the flow of kundalini energy.

When awakened through right living i.e., not wasting the procreative essences, not allowing your body to become acidic or toxified by stress hormones and you are able to maintain a balance between the sympathetic and parasympathetic nervous system, the kundalini rises through the sushumna nadi, following the path of the terminal filament.

The only evidence I have found over many years of research for this 13-month time frame is in Harold Percival's book "Thinking and Destiny". So, if you'd like to learn more I recommend starting there. Percival claims that if thirteen lunar cycles are successfully completed, the terminal filament which is usually clogged in adults reopens, creating a direct path for the "seed" from the base of the spine, coccygeal body (kundalini gland) to the cerebellum and so on. He also describes the many changes that occur in the body due to the terminal filament being restored. I won't share the details here as it's very complex and would double the size of this book!

The conclusion of the entire process is that the biochemicals of super consciousness, (the great regeneration or sacred secretion) enhance consciousness, cognitive abilities, and health along all lines. Since healing and success are intrinsically intwined, you also become a powerful magnet for your dreams and desires.

An added benefit is the reinvigoration of the long-term memory powered by the hippocampus; this is known as "accessing the book of life, akashic record or DNA blueprint" -- it's the recollection of the true self.

For those who have experienced severe trauma, the reinvigoration of the long-term memory can be challenging, however it does give you the opportunity to reflect, process old wounds and gain true closure and healing.

> The Hippocampus is a primary region for neurogenesis (mind generation and renewal), it contains multipotent neural stem cells. Neurogenesis in the hippocampus literally gives the opportunity to create new brain cells (neurons) and become empowered with new inspiration and new ideas. Hence the Scripture, *"Be transformed by the renewing of your mind."* **Romans 12:2.**

Warning, once you have gained heightened awareness the world you are living in can seem very different, some individuals find this very jarring and struggle to reintegrate with their newfound knowledge. Having the ability to remember the fine details from our young lives and even past lives can be a lot to accept. Of course, it is difficult to accept the things that have hurt and scarred us, but acceptance and forgiveness of self and other in the past and present is very liberating, plus you finally break the chains that have been holding you back. In acceptance and forgiveness, you are literally giving to your future – forward-giving! Heightened intuition to see beyond the lies of society can also be a lot to take on board. This is why I've produced YouTube videos that include practices to help you remain in bliss and realise the power you hold. Hold fast, embrace the changes, accept, and give thanks at every juncture and the bliss will cascade through your life and being!

THE PROCESS 10
A Full Summary of the Inner Alchemical Process

There is a perpetual cycle occurring in the temple body. The cycle can cause degeneration or regeneration physically, mentally, and spiritually depending on our vibration and choices.

The regeneration of the fluidic (lunar) body happens monthly, coinciding with the moon.

The regeneration of the mineral (solar) body happens yearly, coinciding with the sun (every 13 moon cycles).

Light in the form of photons (electromagnetic energy) is received by the brain which precipitates in the body as cerebrospinal fluid (CSF) and is then differentiated by the pineal and pituitary.

The two potencies (pineal and pituitary) flow through the autonomic nervous system, through the semilunar ganglion and into the solar plexus where they merge and conceive the seed in the spleen.

After conception some of the seed will automatically flow up the spinal cord from T12, Percival calls this "automatic reclaiming".

The remainder enters the vagus nerve and descends to the procreative organs where it is further vivified (if not expelled).

Through what Percival calls "voluntary reclaiming", the vivified seed is then reabsorbed into the body where it begins its ascension to C_4 for the baptism.

On its path to C_4 it travels through other vital organs including the kidneys and the heart. Love in the heart stimulates oxytocin release by the pituitary, this chemical is the catalyst for pineal metabolism.

After its baptism by thyroxine the seed arrives at the double cross of Ida and Pingala and the vagus nerve where it is crucified.

After crucifixion the seed is sent to the tomb (cerebellum).

The cerebellum admits the "resurrected" seed through the cerebellar lingula, into the fourth ventricle (CSF reservoir), where it is distributed into CSF, the pituitary and the pineal via the posterior commissure.

This causes the pituitary to secrete floods of oxytocin and vasopressin which consequently invigorates the pineal.

The stimulated pineal glows rich with nitric oxide, closing the circuit between these two major endocrine glands. The pineal then upgrades melatonin to **DMT and the other biochemicals of super consciousness.**

The enhanced CSF is "Amrita -- the nectar of the Gods" -- magnetized and charged (**ionized).

Thanks to the spirit-fire catalyst (nitric oxide) CSF is multiplied and flooded with DMT, pinoline, and the other biochemicals of super consciousness.

Immediately after, the process will begin again... and again...

Each cycle permits some of the essence to descend the central CSF canal via the ventricles, thus the temple body is purified by degree.

After the thirteenth round the hollow through the terminal filament (sushumna) is said to be fully cleared, thus the seed can travel directly from the coccygeal body to the brain.

The biochemicals of the great regeneration (sacred secretion) are healing and rejuvenating like nothing else, also enhancing consciousness, cognitive abilities, the higher senses and health along all lines.

This entire process is affected by two major INPUTS – outside in and inside out!

The outcomes of chosen inputs will always be reflected in our bodies and circumstances.

PRACTICAL GUIDANCE

HOW TO RAISE THE SACRED SECRETION – THE PRACTICAL SIDE OF ACTIVATING KUNDALINI ENERGY AND CHARGING CSF (CHRIST OIL)

This section of the book is dedicated to the practical aspects of preserving and raising the sacred secretion in which, specific guidelines, practices, and methods will be given.

If you want to take your practice a step further, I have a course available on the **Teach:able** platform/website called, "**Super Consciousness Awakening.**" It provides further practical guidance and insight to realising the alchemical transformation for yourself. This course is designed to really deepen your understanding, recognise the keys that you hold and consciously manifest your own radiant transformation!

PRACTICAL GUIDANCE INTRO – EXTERIOR INPUTS AND INTERIOR INPUTS

There are two major inputs that anyone seeking to preserve and raise the sacred secretion should be aware of and seek to govern like a loving caretaker.

1. EXTERIOR INPUTS
(What we allow to affect any or all levels of our being from the **outside in**).

- Food
- Drink
- Media
- Human influence
- Environment

2. INTERIOR INPUT
(What we allow to affect any or all levels of our being from the **inside out**).

- Thought
- Emotion
- Sensations

Since everything listed here affect our thoughts, emotions, habits, and behaviours they subsequently affect our vibratory frequency and biochemistry. This is why all of these inputs should be considered and managed, especially during your sacred secretion or super consciousness awakening practice time.

All of the above inputs come under seven simple guidelines, principles, or fundamentals for awakening the super consciousness:

1. Food and Water.
2. Attitude, State of Mind, and Influence.
3. Sunlight.
4. Air (Breathwork) and Meditation.
5. Sleep and Relaxation.
6. Exercise.
7. Preservation of Procreative Essences.

The following chapters will explain these inputs and principles in detail in order for you to easily apply them for yourself.

FOOD AND DRINK:

Your "exterior inputs" include the foods and drinks that you choose to consume. Saliva affects pH and the mineral content of your "living waters"; acidic pH diminishes your ability to regenerate.

Therefore, doing A) A Juice Fast, or B) The Daniel Fast (NATURAL vegan diet) for the duration of your practice are good ways to optimise, purify and support ALL of your vital systems. Ideally you should consume an alkaline diet **all** the time, not just when the moon is in your sun sign and avoid toxins wherever possible.

I have shared very specific recipes for specific Sacred Secretion smoothies on my YouTube Channel "Kelly-Marie Kerr", each one can assist your practice and transformation marvellously.

If you opt for the Juice Fast method, I recommend the following regime:

1. Banana and Onion Chakra Cleanse each morning (see YouTube for recipe).
2. Limitless Alkalising pH water throughout the day (see YouTube for recipe).
3. Nitic Oxide Booster at lunch time (see YouTube for recipe).
4. Nitric Oxide Booster at teatime

5. Banana Tryptophan DMT Tea (see YouTube for recipe) before bed (not immediately before though as you don't want to be up all night going back and forward from the loo)!

This regime is carefully curated and specifically designed to ensure that your body is in a prime position to feel the benefits of your practice, but EVERYONE is different, and you should consider what your intuition tells you will be best for you.

If you opt for the Daniel Fast Method, a typical day could be the same as a juice fast day with some additions:

1. Banana and Onion Chakra Cleanse each morning.
2. Over-night oats
3. Limitless Alkalising pH water throughout the day
4. Nitic Oxide Booster at lunch time
5. Chickpea and walnut Salad
6. Soup with Ezekiel bread
7. Banana Tryptophan DMT Tea before bed (not immediately before though as you don't want to be up all night going back and forward from the loo)!

Again, you'll need to adapt these ideas to suit your own needs, taste preferences and hunger levels because you might find the juices more filling than you imagine, or vice versa.

Just remember, there's no iron-clad structure – you can take and leave what you like form these guidelines, if you're hungry on the juice fast grab something like celery sticks and houmous, or sliced apples with organic nut butter, there are always options and it's good to be prepared before your practice time begins!

Daniel Fast Context:

The Daniel fast is a natural, plant-based diet with NO processed foods, NO caffeine, and NO alcohol allowed. For the rest of the month, just do your best to limit the meat, processed foods, caffeine, and alcohol that you consume.

The "Daniel Fast" is renowned as a way to honour "God" and complement our prayers. In the Bible, the "Daniel" fast kept the metaphorical lions at bay and gave Daniel *"understanding in all his visions and dreams."* **Daniel 1:17 (KJV)**

12-16 Hour Over-night Fast:

It is also beneficial to leave at least a 12 to 16-hour gap between your last and first meal of the day. This will reduce carbon dioxide, raise nitric oxide, and assist pineal metabolism. For example, if you eat dinner at 6pm do not have breakfast until at least 6am. You can have as much water, infused water, and caffeine free tea in between as you like.

> *"The reduction of food intake increased melatonin levels in all tissues investigated, particularly in the stomach and the brain."*
> **The Journal of Pineal Research [January 1992] By G.A Bubenik, R.O Ball and S.F Pang**

Excess carbon dioxide in the body is highly detrimental in a multitude of ways. Alchemists referred to carbon dioxide as "fixed air" and knew that it in excess it inhibits the inner process. Carbon dioxide is produced in the body during digestion. Therefore, fasting or eating only when you are truly hungry reduces carbon dioxide in the body.

In particular eating highly acidic, low karma, processed foods and meat will raise carbon dioxide levels.

Other Substances Context:

Cigarettes, marijuana, and other recreational drugs or mind-altering substances (no matter how "natural") do of course alter your biological and biochemical balance, hormone secretions and circulation and will therefore interfere with this inner alchemical process. Some of these substances might indeed be "good" for you but should not be used at all on your sacred secretion days.

**Side note – Do you best to never smoke anything at all! Your throat is your power centre and your lungs are your wings!

Potential Hydrogen (pH Level) Context:

In the body, there is a perpetual exchange occurring between blood, CSF, sexual vital essences, and lymph – all of these fluids are directly affected by what we eat.

> "No drunkard can inherit the Kingdom of Heaven, for acids and alcohol cut, or chemically split, the oil that unites with the mineral salts in the body to produce the monthly seed."
> **Page 90, "God Man: The Word Made Flesh" by George W. Carey and Ines Eudora Perry.**

A HEALTHY body is incredibly efficient at keeping our pH levels normal (7.35-7.45) and it's at this normal level that our cells can function properly:

- Above 7.45 the body will be in metabolic alkalosis.
- Below 7.35 the body will be in a state of metabolic acidosis.

pH stands for potential hydrogen and refers to the number of electrons (life force) available in the fluidic body. Neutral or slightly alkaline pH means that there are plenty of free electrons in the body. Acidic pH means that the body has electron deficit.

The acidity and alkalinity of our food massively raises and lowers the body's natural pH level. Symptoms of acidosis are headaches, lethargy, weakness, stiffness, fatigue, breathing difficulties, confusion, and anxiety.

To maintain a balanced pH your body pulls minerals (cell salts), such as potassium, sodium, calcium, and magnesium from tissues in order to neutralize acid in the blood. Kidney's filter excess acid out of the body through urine, so you can imagine how hard the poor kidneys must have to work if our diets are extremely acidic. Although our bodies are brilliantly designed to regulate our pH, it is up to us to assist it by honouring our bodies with clean alkaline-producing foods.

Due to prominent levels of acidity in animal products our bodies will naturally be more balanced when following a vegan diet. Over-eating, eating too much processed acidic food and or drinking alcohol will limit the potential of awakening the super consciousness.

Hydration Context:

Hydration is everything, so drink plenty of good quality water. At least 3 litres per day. Watch out for pH levels in bottled water, try to drink water that is pH 7 or above.

Untouched water in its natural habitat (source) is high-alkaline (usually pH 9+) and is rich in minerals. Water in this state would naturally assist in the maintenance, restoration, and regeneration of the boy with its high electron and mineral presence.

Since the body is made up of 70% water, a wonderful way to assist the inner alchemical process is by encouraging our body's pH level to remain neutral, this can be done by drinking water that is infused with alkalising foods.

Since the water available through our taps and shops has been highly processed and or distilled for purification, it is extremely difficult to access water with a natural pH of 9+. So, after a lot of reading and experimentation, I now use a combination of lemon, ginger, cinnamon, and pink Himalayan salt in my water. This recipe is also available as a video "Alkalising Power Water" on my YouTube channel.

Alkalising Power Water Recipe

There is no need to be specific about how much of each ingredient you add to your water. Just make sure the ingredients are rinsed thoroughly, then use a large jug or container to make the drink and keep it refrigerated between use.

*Chop a few lemons into quarters, squeeze the juice into your jug of water and then add the lemon peel to your water also.

1. Lemon is a strong antioxidant and immune system (lymph) booster.
2. Lemons are amniotic, producing alkaline by-products when metabolised.

3. The scent of lemon releases pheromones and oxytocin (the catalyst for pineal metabolism)

*Either pop a few Ceylon cinnamon sticks straight into your jug of water or add a few spoons of powder.

1. Cinnamon improves Insulin sensitivity (remember insulin
supports DNA gene expression)

*Peel and chop a large ginger root and put the pieces in your water.

1. Ginger stimulates the circulation.
2. Ginger is a powerful antioxidant and purifier of vital fluids.
3. Ginger clears the endocrine glands and helps your body to carry
nutrients to the places that need healing the most.

*Add 1-2 teaspoons of ground pink Himalayan salt to your water.
- Salt is a conductor of electricity and has the ability to increase
your piezoelectric charge. But regular "table salt" is stripped of the
many other minerals which are present in pink Himalayan salt. Pink
Himalayan Salt will also support Iodine levels in the body. Iodine
is an electron donor and makes ATP and energy. It is the activator
of all vital bodily functions. A healthy Iodine balance in the body
is essential for a favourable bio-electrical vibration.

Deficient iodine levels can wreak havoc on our bodies (including causing c***** development and growth). Simply put, Iodine is
integral, dynamic, and AMAZING but, be sure to do your own
research as certain types of iodine are harmful. Iodine is found
EVERYWHERE in the body it is: Anti-microbial, anti-bacterial,

anti-mucus, anti-parasitic, a brain function supporter, anti-viral and an immune system booster. It also helps to decalcify the pineal gland.

Alkalinity and De-calcifying Context:

Just as a showerhead or shower door can clearly be seen to become calcified by what we call "lime scale" from fluoride in water and other calcifying agents, the body and pineal gland can become calcified from acidosis and fluoride. The primary principle for living a long, healthy life is keeping all of the channels within the body free from the coatings of "lime" (calcification). Clean alkalising foods (organic even more so) assist in clarifying the body, which includes optimising Pineal function and subsequently Pituitary and Thalamic functions.

Thomas Burgoyne put it like this,

> "Every vein and canal throughout the entire body, from youth to maturity, is being coated with carbonate of lime, or lime in some form (known as calcification). The coatings of the walls of the veins in such a manner, prevents the circulation of living matter; then, the real vitality of the food which we eat, is simply passed through the pores, or through the bowels, because it is unable to penetrate through the lime."
>
> **Page 67 [Alchemy] "The Light of Egypt" by Thomas H. Burgoyne**

Top 10 foods for decalcification and a balanced pH:

1. Spinach
2. Lime
3. Kale

4. Avocados
5. Wheatgrass
6. Celery
7. Broccoli
8. Cucumber
9. Bell Peppers
10. Garlic

A great way to view the best sources of edible energy is by looking at the "Karmic Food Pyramid" in which foods are scored by their energetic composition and by physical levels of vitamins and minerals.

For example, Chlorophyll is at the top of the Karmic Food Pyramid because, like sunlight, it is abundant to produce, regenerative in its composition and has a pH balancing effect on the body. At the bottom of the pyramid are things like processed meat because it is very acidic, not to mention the fact that, they have widely been injected with synthesised hormones which wreak havoc on the body.

> "When the whole of this mighty scheme is taken into consideration, students will see how necessary it is for those who wish to develop their spiritual possibilities to live upon a purely vegetable diet, because the eating of flesh attracts the soul to the animal kingdom and degrades the higher senses."
> **(Page 75) [Mediumship – Its Nature and Mysteries] "The Light of Egypt" by Thomas H Burgoyne**

ATTITUDE STATE OF MIND AND INFLUENCE:

Several of the exterior and interior inputs like media, human influence and environment come under this heading and a lot of the practical application methods will easily fall into place when we're thinking and feeling positive, so let's explore.

Emotions

Emotions are vibratory frequencies (wavelengths) and are ultimately what cause all the biological and biochemical activity within the body.

The vibratory frequencies produced by having a disposition of love, calmness, joy, and gratitude will assist the pituitary gland with oxytocin and vasopressin release, which in turn facilitates pineal metabolism (melatonin upgrades).

Strong, negative emotions such as anger, fear, anxiety, or guilt cause the body to secrete chemicals such as cortisol that oppose pineal metabolism.

Words are also vibratory frequencies (wavelengths) be they positive (high vibration) or negative (low vibration). All words affect emotions, both the things we tell ourselves and the words we say to others. Therefore, a sort of perpetuating circle occurs -- reaction (expressed emotion), biochemical alteration, thought (negative/positive), words (negative/positive) and so on. Be wise; pronounce nothing evil and only good will come. God is good and God is ALL, therefore ALL IS GOOD. This is Eden consciousness. *"If thine eye shall be single, then thy whole body shall be filled with light."*

Calm, balanced responses from the heart centre aids the inner alchemical process of enlightenment. Pause when you're in a trigger situation and don't be afraid to ask for time -- just say "I don't know how I feel about that right now," or "I need to process what you've just said." Particularly during your practice time, aim to spend time in solitude where you have space to hear the inner voice and kindly avoid of people who trigger negative (fearful or stressful) alterations in your biochemistry.

Aim to be in peaceful environments, you may have to go to work, care for elderly/difficult family members and or children so it's impossible to avoid all emotional and stressful triggers completely but that's fine! Your best is all that's required and even the smallest amount of progress towards balance and empathetic compassion counts.

Try to find the upside of every situation and accept life's lessons as they come. Make the decision to be balanced rather than negative, calm rather than explosive, kind rather than aggressive etc. As the saying goes: "It is better to light a candle than to curse the darkness."

Use affirmations like, I am loving, I am loved, I am love and I am gracious, I am grateful, and I am grace. Ask the God power IN and THROUGH you to help you feel true love and grace.

Too much negative emotion keeps the body in sympathetic (fight or flight) mode, and we get so busy trying to "survive" that parasympathetic (rest and digest) functions can't take place. Ultimately this causes imbalance.

Again, each "emotion" has a vibratory frequency (wavelength) that slots somewhere into the spectrum between the extremes of love and fear. Fear has a long, slow vibratory frequency whereas love has a high, rapid vibratory frequency.

Long, slow fear-based vibrations inhibit us from activating the 64 possible codes of amino acids of DNA. Presently humans have approximately 20 active codes (20 amino acids) of the 64. This is due to switches at the coding sites turning on and off in reaction to manifested emotions. This is a hard link between emotion and human genetics. Long, slow fearful frequencies render the coding sites less active than high, rapid love-based frequencies which have more potential sites for coding along the genetic pattern.

Reactive or animalistic (carnal) emotions inhibit you from reaching an enlightened state of consciousness. Hence why the Bible says, "the carnal mind is enmity (opposition) against God" **Romans 8:7 (KJV)**.

Try to take advice or correction objectively without irrational and reactive defensiveness, resentment, or rebellion. You are not in competition with anyone or anything – YOUR PERSONAL BEST IS ALL THAT COUNTS.

Try to accept neglect without hurt or insult. Let go of your need to refer to yourself during conversations, or to continually announce your successes. You are not in competition with anyone or anything – YOUR PERSONAL BEST IS ALL THAT COUNTS. Do good work that benefits others and you'll soon reap the benefits.

Try to be content, take time to appreciate every blessing big and small. Forget what is missing and relish what you already have. You'll be surprised at how this matches your own vibratory frequency to that of abundance and thus opens the door for wonders and miracles.

Refuse to let anger rise in your heart. Due to heavy, negative conditioning, social programming and fear mongering the majority of people humanity is greatly flawed – love people anyway and accept them if they don't agree with you. You are not here to worry about or change anybody else – THEIR SHORT FALLS ARE NOT YOUR BUSINESS.

Not everyone has the awareness or conscience to live by the same standards as you. Rules get bent and hearts get broken. Don't react with carnal reflexes, all challenges can be endured with quiet, self-comforting reflection, diplomacy, and loving wisdom.

Be free -- float above every base-level annoyance that has the potential to rob you of your peace and joy and inhibit you from reaching your own goals. You are an eagle reaching for the heavens on a high altitude, not a pigeon pecking around in scraps of waste.

Parasympathetic and Sympathetic Balance Context:

Maintaining a balance between the parasympathetic (rest and digest) and sympathetic (fight of flight) nervous systems is paramount. You need spend enough time in rest and digest each day, so that the body has time to regenerate.

Sympathetic nervous system dominance can result in a whole host of problems including obesity, abnormally slow heartbeat, difficulty swallowing, gastrointestinal diseases, fainting, mood disorders, B12 deficiency, chronic inflammation, and seizures. This can all occur because the basic, necessary bodily functions such as digestion, circulation and blood purification become restricted when we are fearful, stressed or even just busy and overwhelmed. This is because the sympathetic nervous system automatically prioritizes survival, keeping you in a state of mania.

The parasympathetic nervous system optimises calmness, healing, and bliss. It puts us in "rest and digest" mode and helps blood and CSF flow to the brain. Parasympathetic nervous system dominance supports creativity, reduces anxiety, and produces clarity by allowing all of the body's systems to work in harmony with one another. Parasympathetic nervous system dominance can even improve the symptoms of conditions such as: heart disease, tinnitus, migraines, alcohol addiction, Alzheimer's, and obesity to name a few!

Let's look at a few easy suggestions for cultivating parasympathetic nervous system dominance. It's no coincidence that these pointers correlate with everything else we've learned so far.

1. Breathing Exercises (pranayama's) – there are some guided videos on my YouTube channel.
2. Showers and Baths (the sensation of water on the body relaxes us and therefore helps the body to switch into the parasympathetic mode).
3. Singing and Humming activates parasympathetic mode (this is why mantras and worship or giving thanks and praise via song are effective spiritual methods).
4. Exercise - growth hormones produced when exercising assist the vagus nerve and the brain's mitochondria thus helping to reverse cognitive decline.
5. Yoga - increases the calming neurotransmitter (GABA) which facilitates parasympathetic nervous system dominance.
6. Massage – especially on the feet and neck stimulates your vagus nerve.

7. Smiling – scientific experiments have demonstrated that smiling stimulates the vagus nerve in a beneficial way.

Natural (Hermetic) Law Context:

It's natural law that every one of our responses and attitudes affects us internally, as well as externally. The Natural Laws are the fundamentals of science. We were created with conscience and compassion in order to feel and recognise the difference between right and wrong. We depend upon God (True Source Love) for absolutely everything, including the air and life force that keeps us alive, thus we should honour the laws of nature to make the world a loving and peaceful place.

The seven principles of Hermeticism, also known as the seven laws of nature, are:

1. **Mentalism** - The understanding that Universal Mind (God) is Infinite.
2. Affirmation: *"God is good, and God is All – therefore All is good."*
3. **Correspondence** - The understanding of Macrocosm (the whole) and microcosm (a part); "As above so below" and "on earth as it in heaven."
4. Affirmation: *"In Spirit and in Truth, I am all that God is."*
5. **Vibration** - The understanding that nothing rests: EVERYTHING is moving.
6. Affirmation: *"Centred in the knowledge of the All presiding good I am not disturbed by illusions."*
7. **Polarity** - The understanding of duality: All relative truths are but half-truths.
8. Affirmation: *"I am whole, complete, balanced and rooted in Love."*

9. **Rhythm** - The understanding that what rises will fall and that which goes out will come in.

10. Affirmation: *"I am consciously aware that every one of my emotions, thoughts and actions has a consequence."*

11. **Cause and Effect** - The understanding that everything happens according to law, nothing ever entirely escapes nature's laws.

12. Affirmation: *"I am the master of my emotions, thoughts and body and I choose to cause good."*

13. **Gender** - Everything has masculine and feminine aspects, including light (electromagnetic energy) and together the aspects manifest EVERYTHING.

14. Affirmation: *"I respect both aspects of myself and am balanced in divine Love."*

There is also one other law, arguably the most empowering and progressive law of all!

1. **Forgiveness and Grace** - The understanding that God (True Source Love/Power), IN and THROUGH us, Loves and forgives unconditionally and without limit.

To master life is to acknowledge the law of cause and effect and thus operate from our Spiritual centre - the Sacred Heart. When the quality of our thoughts improves and the choice of language that we use enhances we become exceedingly powerful at recognising and seizing the many wonderful opportunities in our midst.

> *"Among our associates, we like and are attracted to those who understand and sympathise with our thoughts. The same law holds good in Divine Mind – its thoughts are drawn to and find*

> *expression in the minds of those who raise themselves to its thought standards."*
> **Charles Fillmore, Prosperity**

Exposure to toxic energies that lower your vibratory frequency are detrimental to the process regardless as to whether you experience them in person or via a screen, so you should avoid watching violent, stressful, sensual, low vibe media (particularly the news) on the television or other devices during your practice time – and preferably at other times too!

When you do feel triggered out of bhakti and or serenity, just breathe, and aim to allow, accept and as much as possible go with life's ebbs and flows – remember, acceptance, compassion and gratitude keep our vibratory frequencies high allowing for oxytocin heart expansions, heart/brain cohesion, CSF multiplication, and pineal metabolism!

Literally EVERYTHING we sense, feel, or perceive affects our vibratory frequency and in turn our lymphatic systems and cellular body. Low frequencies diminish our ability to regenerate.

GETTING PRACTICAL AND DELIBERATE ABOUT MAINTAINING YOUR VIBE:

- You are the director of your thoughts, so keep them high vibe – until this becomes second nature, or habitual you can set timers if you need to remind yourself to reside in acceptance, gratitude, peace, and love.

- Practice praise (gratitude) by singing songs and mantras that synchronise the hemispheres of your brain and cause deep heart brain resonance.
- Pray openly and freely, set your intentions, offload – list what you're grateful for – reside in a place of connection with the divine. List what you'd like to release and carefully burn the paper the list is written on.
- You are the director of your emotions, so flow like water – breathe and let everything discordant slip away freely.
- Use guided positive affirmation videos or even write your own affirmations and use those also.
- Use meditations that allow space for new thought patterns to emerge, I recommend the "Healing and Success are One: Part 3" video on my YouTube channel for this purpose.
- Use meditations and breath exercises such as the ones on my YouTube channel that help to release old thought, emotion, habits, addictions, and sensation programmes.

SUNLIGHT

Sunlight comes under the input of "environment." Make sure you receive daily exposure to NATURAL light; photon energy is imperative to the overall health of the cellular terrain.

It doesn't have to be a bright and sunny day and you don't need to be half naked – a simple 15-minute walk with your head and neck exposed to daylight is fantastic for vitamin D and nitrogen/phosphorus absorption for serotonin production.

AIR (BREATHWORK) AND MEDITATION

Breath is an underlying principle beneath all of the inputs. It's a subconscious mechanism, but our breath patterns change according to our various different states of being. Stress induces shallow breathing, whereas joy allows the breath to flow more freely.

Meditation and breath exercises help shift the body into parasympathetic (rest and digest) mode for healing and regeneration. As stated in the lesson on DMT -- deep, nourishing breaths can reduce carbon dioxide in the blood thus facilitating pineal metabolism.

Breathing exercises also help to encourage the piezoelectric function of the pineal by increasing CSF flow. The increased flow stimulates calcite crystal vibration and enhances pineal metabolism.

Meditation improves the flow of CSF and other vital fluids through the body by calming the glands in the brain and allowing the lower and upper CSF pumps to work in harmony with one another. In fact, scientists have found that during sleep there is as much as a 60% increase of CSF which aids melatonin enhancements.

Furthermore, meditation is a means of allowing the left and right brains to synchronise, this is known as hemi-syncing which helps in producing vibratory frequencies that allow increased levels of DHEA's, heart centre activation (oxytocin release), and melatonin secretions.

The slowing of the brain waves is what causes our consciousness to leave the analytical brain and move into the autonomic nervous system thereby accessing the subconscious operating system. The longer we can reside in a place of stillness and peace the more efficient the brain becomes at purifying, strengthening, regenerating, and healing us - body, mind, and spirit.

Scientific studies show that Melatonin levels in the body peak between 1am and 4am. This is a prime time for pineal metabolism to synthesize DMT and the biochemicals of super consciousness, this is why yogis do their practice at dawn.

GETTING PRACTICAL:

- Take time to breathe deeply; even five minutes of deep nostril breathing each day will improve your health along all lines.
- Try diaphragm breathing, such as is used in the practise of Kundalini, which activates the CSF sacral pump at the bottom of the spine. This occurs as the dome shaped diaphragm muscle contracts down on the sacrum on an in breath, which pumps CSF up the spinal cord and into the brain. A succession of these contractions stimulates both pumps and encourages or strengthens their ability after the practice. I have a video called Guided CSF Meditation on my YouTube channel to help you.
- Meditating (focusing) on the Pineal gland can assist with melatonin upgrades and the secretion of the biochemicals of super consciousness awakening.
- Meditating on the things you are most grateful for, by sitting and breathing deeply whilst making an invisible list of all your blessings will raise your vibratory frequency in no time.

Challenge yourself to do this every night as you are falling asleep and note the effect it has.

It's kind of old school and certainly not for everyone, but I like meditating on the prayer of Jabez, *"Oh, that you would bless me indeed, and enlarge my territory, that your hand would be with me, and that you would keep me from evil, that I may not cause pain"* 1 Chronicles 4:10 (KJV) I like to read it out loud 5 times, then silently in my head 5 times and then close my eyes and breathe whilst thinking about it for 5 minutes. The outcome is wonderful.

Biblically, those who took the time to listen and hear the inner voice of God (Super Consciousness) were blessed; Joshua, Isaac and Luke are among those who mention the worth of meditation and Mary was blessed because she sat still and listened.

Silence is truly a virtue. Silent meditation allows us to discern and hear the Super Conscious voice and to purify or renew the mind. Find a quiet spot and choose a focal point in your mind's eye, I like to use the word "love" or "light". Then begin to breathe slowly. If your mind starts to wander and you find yourself thinking about the thoughts of the day, simply bring it back to stillness by repeating "light" or "love" silently until the thoughts melt away. It will get easier to remain focused and soon you'll become brilliant at creating peace and silence in your mind.

There are many other ways to meditate, and I encourage you to find a method that suits your personal preferences.

SLEEP AND RELAXATION

Sleep is also an underlying principle that will help you master all of the interior and exterior inputs. Getting 7-8 hours sleep is paramount for life, health, and super consciousness awakening. There are several reasons for this:

- Thyroxine purifies the body during sleep.
- The parasympathetic nervous system is fully active during sleep.
- CSF (Christ Oil) actually clears energetic thought debris during sleep.

If you are restless or have difficulty sleeping, do not worry. Just spending your nights laying in a comfortable position and meditating on all the things you are grateful for will induce the benefits of relaxation. The key is not to get frustrated but accept and meet yourself exactly where you're at.

Stillness and peace can be induced by silently repeating "I am Light," or "Sat Chit Ananda" and imagining the light within you increasing.

EXERCISE

Exercise is a gift and another underlying principle of health, wellness, and a high-vibratory frequency! Your body was made to move, it likes to move... movement creates energy, nitric oxide, ATP, and has many other benefits. So, dance, walk, do yoga, run, cartwheel whatever you like – just make sure you get your heart rate up for a minimum of 20 minutes daily.

Quickened breathing patterns for nitric oxide production, carbon dioxide elimination and effective CSF circulation are the most effective methods of pineal activation and health. This is the science behind the kundalini "breath of fire." Therefore, any activity that increases your heart rate (and consequently breathing rhythm) will assist you in these areas.

Most types of exercise have a positive effect on the human body. Exercise increases strength, facilitates the metabolism and circulatory systems, and in turn conditions the blood and CSF which, as we have seen, are integral facilitators in awakening super consciousness.

Yoga is particularly good for people with any level of fitness and works because it facilitates the flow of CSF and the generation of nitric oxide through the body. Not to mention increasing lymphatic activity.

The scholars who translated the Dead Sea Scrolls, owned by the Essenes also known as the "perfect light race", found that the earliest forms of "Christianity" were based on the yogic teachings of the Essenes. The Essenes were dedicated to perfecting their bodies and souls to become more angelic, in hope of restoring peace on Earth!

There are 33 yoga videos available to paying members of my YouTube channel "Kelly-Marie Kerr" inspired by Essene Yoga. You can make your own custom yoga playlists with these videos – so your practice can be as long or short as you like, and you can make the focus whatever asanas you fancy.

The "Essene Way" also known as "Essene Yoga" includes several yogic traditions -- **Hatha, Bhakti, Jnana, Karma, Mantra, Laya, and Raja.**

Hatha is also expressed as "Asana and Pranayama" meaning movement and breath. The primary focus of Hatha Yoga is building control of the physical body – which in turn increases strength, circulation, resolve and determination of the mind.

Bhakti is a thankful and loving disposition. "The Essene Way" teaches us to approach Yoga and life in a state of Bhakti, so that we look for love and beauty in ALL things. The flow of CSF and nerve fluid within the body can be blocked by any external force that overcomes or shocks the body's internal ability to adapt to it (trauma). The free flow of mental impulses relating to CSF flow in the central nervous system is vital. So, deal with things and then let them go.

Karma yoga is all about serving -- nurturing ourselves and others through our emotions, thoughts, and actions.

Jnana yoga has to do with knowledge and the expansion of knowingness (gnosis). The knowledge that is obtained by asking ourselves questions such as, "What is my purpose?" and "Who or what is God?" To which we may find the answers in sacred holy texts or deep in meditation.

Mantra Yoga uses the power of the spoken word and its vibratory frequencies to manifest peace, light and love in ourselves and the world we live in.

Raja pertains to transcending mind beyond attachment to carnal (matter-limited) understanding. It is silent meditation time that allows us to hear God's "still small voice" and make space for God's vision in our lives.

Laya Yoga is present in all yogic traditions and pertains to the use of our breath. The Greek word for Spirit is "Pneuma" and it literally means breath and wind. Like Kundalini, Laya acknowledges the subtle energy of the Chakras and their coinciding physical glands. It focuses on raising the vibratory frequencies within the body. In advanced lessons, Laya Yoga is also used to develop total authority over our senses.

Within the examination of these 7 yogic disciplines, we can see that breath, movement, sound, and meditation all work together to help physical, emotional, mental, and spiritual blockages to dissolve.

All 33 of the videos included in channel membership incorporate the aspects of the Essene Way.

PRESERVATION OF PROCREATIVE ESSENCES

Each month, when the moon is in your zodiac refrain from climax induced by any sort of sexual stimulation. You should completely abstain from sexual activity during this time, including looking or thinking about sexually arousing images. Don't get frustrated if your mind wanders into these realms, just be aware of your urges and return your focus to the higher chakras – energy follows thought, so you can easily reshift your energy upward. The commercial world thrives by keeping the energy of the population locked in their lower centres with their erotic music videos, sugar laden temptations, and other more extreme lures! The world seems geared toward having people unwittingly draw the vital essences downward instead of encouraging them to flow upward for increased consciousness awakening and enlightenment. It's not that sex is a "sin" per say, but there must be a balance.

When the Bible talks about *"separating the sheep from the goats"*, it is highlighting the importance of leading with your head centre (Aries) and not letting carnal desire stemming from the sacral centre (Capricorn or Goat) lead you astray.

- CSF ventricles are shaped like a sheep or ram's head (Aries) with its curling horns.
- The procreative organs resemble a goat.

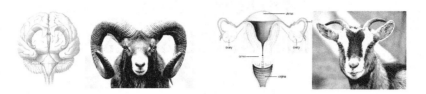

Ventricles and procreative organs.

The subject of retention is explained in more depth in **The God Design: Secrets of the Mind, Body and Soul** and **Elevation: The Divine Power of the Human Body.** There are also several videos about this topic on my YouTube channel, "Kelly-Marie Kerr."

PREPARATION – GETTING READY FOR THE MOON TO ENTER YOUR SUN SIGN

With a deeper understanding of the steps required to optimise your practise, here is a quick list of tips that will help you be prepared for your individual time-phase.

1. Get a moon tracking App such as **Deluxe Moon** or purchase **The ReGENEration Calendar or Sacred Secretion Timing Calendar from amazon.**
2. Use the App/Calendar to find out when the moon will next be moving into your zodiac sign as per the instructions in chapter of this book titled: **THE PROCESS PART 1: The Timing and Quality of the Monthly Influx, "When the moon enters your zodiac sign."**
3. Once you know when to do your sacred secretion/regeneration practice, you should create as much time and space for yourself as possible (yes, I know that our lives are hectic). Just try not to book anything in on these days unless you have to!
4. Work and certain celebrations can't be avoided but going for drinks after work probably can, so do your best to free up your calendar.

5. This will help you to avoid temptations, trigger situations, places and or people that you know antagonise.

6. Go shopping, have a good idea of what you'll eat and when and even prepare some meals if time allows. The more prepared you are, the easier your practice will be.

3 Great Breakfast examples:

- Any fresh fruit (not canned) with organic coconut yoghurt.
- Any fresh fruit and or veg smoothie.
- Ezekiel bread with plant butter or organic nut butter.

3 Great Lunch examples:

- Any kind of vegan soup that is free from additives and preservatives.
- Any plant-based sandwich made with Ezekiel bread.
- Any plant-based salad i.e., white bean, chickpea, kidney bean.

3 Great Dinner examples:

- Any kind of lentil, bean and or fresh veg curry with rice.
- Vegan sausages (free from additives and preservatives) with sweet potato wedges or mash.
- Any kind of lentil, bean and or fresh veg stew.

3 Great Snack examples:

- Celery and or carrot sticks with organic houmous.
- Apple slices with organic peanut butter.

- A handful of organic, unsalted nuts (if you need to add salt, do it yourself with organic pink Himalayan or organic Sea salt and a drop of olive oil)

  **Always have a snack or two packed with you when you are on the go, this will stop you from buying junk food on the spare of the moment
  **Always bring a bottle of lemon water or other infused water with you everywhere you go
  **If you have to go to a restaurant, choose a vegan option
  **If you have to go to a bar or club, try having a virgin Mary (filling and delicious)

1. Place a notepad and pen next to your bed, some of your best insights will come at night or upon awakening.

2. Map out a rough schedule for yourself to follow, you don't need to be too precious about this, but it will prepare your mind for what's to come.

3. On your schedule include time for yoga or another form of exercise that raises your heart rate, prayer or meditation time (this can be as simple as sitting still and taking deep nasal breaths for 10 mins twice a day or use the videos offered on my YouTube channel), and replace your TV, phone scrolling time with reading (books that explore spiritual topics help your energies rise to your higher chakras and expand your consciousness).

4. Enjoy your practise days, allow them to be a retreat from overly engaging with the outside world – "for the Kingdom of God is WITHIN you!" Luke 17:21

Namaste x

BOOKS AND PLATFORMS CREATED BY THE AUTHOR KELLY-MARIE KERR

BOOKS:

- **Christ Within, Heaven on Earth**

A concise description of the journey of the glorious sacred secretion (transcript of True anointing YouTube video).

- **The God Design, Secrets of the Body, Mind and Soul**

A thorough study and explanation of both the spiritual and physical elements that form the phenomena known as the sacred secretion. With insights into many of its religious and scientific guises. **Including the full details of the biochemicals of enlightenment.**

- **Elevation, The Divine Power of the Human Body**

The Bible book of Revelation explains the true science of enlightenment: body, mind, and soul in a dramatic, fantastical, and epic parable only 22 chapters. Elevation debunks the symbols and myths providing truth and clarity to its reader.

- **The Cell of Life, Awakening and Regenerating**

A full disclosure of the *3-Fold Enlightenment* or *Great Regeneration*, revealing the scientific parallel of the "Jesus" seed born in the body every lunar month. The "seed" is our opportunity for TOTAL renewal and regeneration.

> *"Every 29.5 days a seed is born in, or out of the solar plexus – the oil unites with the mineral salts and thus produces the monthly seed which goes into the vagus."*
> **Page 90, GOD MAN: The Word Made Flesh by G W Carey**

- **Regeneration Calendar, Keep Track of your Sacred Secretion Times**

A full year calendar providing the sidereal and tropical dates for the moon entering each star sign (zodiac), plus guidelines and meditation techniques to help you on your journey.

PLATFORMS:

- YouTube channel, "Kelly-Marie Kerr" – paid membership gives access to 33 Essene Yoga exercises.
- Websites, *www.seekvision.co.uk* and *www.sacredsecretion.com*
- TikTok, @seekvision
- Instagram, @seekvision
- Facebook, @seekvision33
- Twitter, @seekvision33
- Patreon, Seek Vision (Kelly-Marie Kerr)

SOURCES AND BIBLIOGRAPHY

BIBLES:

"The King James Bible Version (KJV)"

"The Holy Megillah Essene Version"

"The Besorah Of Yahusha Natsarim Bible Version (BYNV)"

"The New International Bible Version (NIV)"

"The Message Bible Version (MSG)"

BOOKS (Alphabetised by surname):

"Healing Mantras" Thomas Ashley-Farrand

"Vol. 1, The anatomy of the human body" C Bell & J Bell

"The Secret Doctrine" Vol 1. Madame Helena P. Blavatsky

"Isis Unveiled: The Secret of The Ancient Wisdom Tradition" Madame P. Blavatsky

"The Kundalini Process" Wim Borsboom

"Conversations on the Edge of the Apocalypse" D J Brown

"The Secretion of Inorganic Phosphate" L. Brull and F. Eichholtz

"The Light of Egypt" Thomas H. Burgoyne

"The Science of The Soul and The Stars" Thomas H. Burgoyne

"The Thymus Gland" M Burnet

"God-Man: The Word Made Flesh" George W. Carey and Ines Eudora Perry

"Relation of The Mineral Salts of The Body to the Signs of The Zodiac" George W. Carey

"The Tree of Life" George W. Carey

"Dictionary of Symbols" J C Cirlot

"The Magic of Water" Masuro Emoto

"Philosophical Transactions Series B, Biological Sciences" Francis Crick and Christof Koch

"The Complete Book of Chakra Healing" Cyndi Dale

"The Twelve Powers of Man" John Fillmore

"Metaphysical Bible Dictionary" Charles Fillmore

"Talks on Truth" Charles Fillmore

"The Doldrums, Christ and the Plantanism" B R Garcia

"The Occult Anatomy of Man" Manly P. Hall

"The Secret Teachings of All Ages" Manly P. Hall

"The Facts of Nutrition" Hilton Hotema

"The Son of Perfection" Hilton Hotema

"The Secret Doctrine of the Rosicrucian's" Magus Incognito

"Light on Yoga" B.K.S. Iyengar

"The Biology of Kundalini" Justin Kerr

"The Perfect Way" Anna Kingsford

"The Gospel of Thomas: The Gnostic Wisdom of Jesus" Jean-Yves Leloup

"Day Spring of Youth" M

"The Cosmic Serpent" Jeremy Narby

"Revelation the book of Unity" J. Sig Paulson & Ric Dickerson

"Thinking and Destiny" Harold W. Percival

"The Living Message" Eugene H. Peterson

"A Beginners Guide to Creating Reality" Ramtha

"Endogenous Light Nexus Theory of Consciousness" Karl Simanonok

"The Rosicrucian Order" R. Swinburne

"Secrets of the Lymphatic System" Dr T. B. Thomas

"The Essenes, the Scrolls, and the Dead Sea" Joan E. Taylor

"Vallalar's Vision of Nuclear Physics" T Thulasiram

"The Perfect Matrimony" Samael Aun Weor

"Practical Magic" Samael Aun Weor

"Esoteric Science Vol 1" J S Williams

ONLINE SOURCES:

- The Metaphysical Dictionary at www.truthunity.com
- Electric Science Magazine
- Strong's concordance at www.biblehub.com
- www.collinsdictionary.com
- www.neuroquantology.com
- *www.researchgate.net*
- www.archive.org